P9-DXL-265

CALGARY PUBLIC LIBRARY

NOV   2013

THE FUTURE OF
CATHOLICISM

ALSO BY MICHAEL COREN

Heresy (2012)

Why Catholics Are Right (2011)

As I See It (2009)

J.R.R. Tolkien: The Man Who Created the Lord of the Rings (2001)

Setting It Right (1996)

The Man Who Created Narnia: The Story of C.S. Lewis (1994)

The Life of Sir Arthur Conan Doyle (1993)

The Invisible Man: The Life and Liberties of H.G. Wells (1993)

Aesthete (1993)

Gilbert: The Man Who Was G.K. Chesterton (1990)

The Outsiders (1985)

Theatre Royal: 100 Years of Stratford East (1985)

MICHAEL COREN

THE FUTURE OF CATHOLICISM

SIGNAL

McCLELLAND
& STEWART

Copyright © 2013 by Michael Coren

Signal is an imprint of McClelland & Stewart,
a division of Random House of Canada Limited,
a Penguin Random House Company

All rights reserved. The use of any part of this publication reproduced, transmitted in any
form or by any means, electronic, mechanical, photocopying, recording, or otherwise, or
stored in a retrieval system, without the prior written consent of the publisher – or, in case
of photocopying or other reprographic copying, a licence from the Canadian Copyright
Licensing Agency – is an infringement of the copyright law.

Library and Archives Canada Cataloguing in Publication
available upon request

ISBN 978-0-7710-2351-4

Library of Congress Control Number: 2013938893

Typeset in Dante by Erin Cooper
Printed and bound in the United States of America

McClelland & Stewart,
a division of Random House of Canada Limited,
a Penguin Random House Company
One Toronto Street
Toronto, Ontario
M5C 2V6
www.randomhouse.com

1 2 3 4 5   17 16 15 14 13

Dedicated to the Corkery Family

CONTENTS

INTRODUCTION

THE VERY TITLE OF THIS BOOK is likely to cause dissent, but then I regard that as a good and not a bad consequence. To paraphrase G.K. Chesterton, the wonderful thing about getting into hot water is that it keeps you so very clean. There are those who will be perplexed, perhaps angry, that I dare to speculate, even question, the future of the Roman Catholic Church; others who are so convinced that Catholicism has no future at all that they will scold me for dipping a few toes into waters they assume polluted to the point of near evaporation. To the former, we can question the future without condescending to the subject. To the latter – to extend the Chestertonian hygiene reference – dirty feet are never a good thing to boast about. The point is, however, that while the Church itself does not and cannot change in its fundamentals, the world around it, and the context in which it exists, is changing all the time. What Catholics need to do and have to do is to explain where the Church is rooted in permanent truth and why it cannot change, and also – and just as boldly – where the Church is indeed in need of reform, why this is the case, and how it can be achieved. When Cardinal Jorge Mario Bergoglio, Archbishop of Buenos Aires, became Pope Francis in March 2013, there were almost six thousand journalists in Rome to cover the Papal election. Some of them reported on the conclave with expertise and empathy, but others – either out of ignorance or just some jaundiced agenda – insisted on asking the same questions again and again, and almost all of these questions centred on the premise and title of this book. Is the Church going to change; will the new Pope be flexible; is Catholicism going to adapt to the times and alter its teaching on same-sex marriage, abortion, contraception, female ordination, celibate clergy, divorce, and so on. Interestingly, the questions centred almost exclusively on moral and sexual issues rather than directly theological topics, and they were almost all based on the stubborn, virtually religious (forgive me) conviction that the Church was wrong, outdated, and in need of fundamental transformation. This book, then, is obliged to answer the following question in its general tone and various clauses: Does the Church need to change, and if so, where? Where it cannot change, why is this so?

Even before the conclave, and as soon as Pope Benedict XVI shocked the world with his announcement that ill health prevented him from continuing in what must be one of the most physically demanding jobs on earth, the *New York Times* editorialist and Pulitzer Prize winner Nicholas Kristof tweeted, "At some point, the church will accept contraception and female and non-celibate priests. Could it be in the next papacy?" Well, Nick, there are three different issues there, and that you lump them all together reveals a certain ignorance of what you are discussing. But to answer you on at least two of them, no, not this papacy nor the one after that nor the one after that. Kristof is an intelligent man, he has been praised for his writing, his mind is alleged to be sharp and focused. But that tweet, so typical of the mood of the time, would be akin to stating shortly after the ending of the Obama presidency that the United States would soon become a province of Canada, or the retiring head of state would become a host on Fox News. The idea that the Church could contradict Scripture and ordain women as priests, for example – remember, the prime role of a Catholic priest is to represent Christ at the Mass – is simply unthinkable, but would simply mean the Catholic Church was no longer the Catholic Church. This is not change but destruction.

Many of the underpinnings to the questions those journalists in Rome and their international counterparts insisted on asking were staggeringly naïve, but in all honesty, they did represent the views of many ordinary non-Catholics and even numerous "sort of" or cafeteria Catholics out there. Answering them can be a little frustrating at times because we would hope, perhaps naïvely, that these critics would have at least a basic understanding of Catholic theology and apologetics. But it is nevertheless, and largely because of this baleful ignorance, that an informed response is absolutely necessary. At the risk of sounding banal or facile, the Pope is the Pope and the Roman Catholic Church is the Roman Catholic Church. There are major commentators and influential pundits who seem to want the Church to be anything other than Catholic and the Pope to be anything other than Papal. Sorry and all that, but the Pope cannot change certain aspects of teaching anymore than he can suddenly decide that Christ is not the Messiah or God not God. It's not a question of changing with the times; good Lord, the times can be bad just as an idea or a person can be bad. We would not have asked a German in 1938 to change with the times! Fashion is by its nature entirely unreliable as a guide to what is true, right, moral, and just. Catholic teaching is not the same as a dinner party opinion or a water-cooler suggestion, and just because it might be difficult to accept does not mean it is impossible to justify or vital to believe. Change, then, is often a euphemism for compromise if not downright surrender. Then again, we have to understand what change actually is. Let's take the example of one of Pope Francis's first public actions, and one that some saw as indicative of their particular fetish for a changing Church.

During his first Easter as Pope, Francis continued to conduct the ancient Maundy Thursday commemoration as he had done as an archbishop in Argentina. Rather than wash the feet of selected people in a church as is usually the case in Rome and elsewhere, he ventured out in public to demonstrate his love for the marginalized and for the ostensibly unloved. He had washed the feet of men dying of AIDS in Buenos Aires, and in Rome as Pope he visited a juvenile detention centre and washed and kissed the feet not only of young offenders, but of two female young offenders, one of them a Serbian Muslim woman. It was a magnificent event, and an example of pristine Christian love. It was also, though, a microcosm of the misunderstanding of the Catholic Church, both by mainstream media and perhaps ultra-conservatives as well. Pope Francis was breaking with a minor tradition, but in the fulfilment of a far greater and more profound one. Only men's feet had been washed in the past, but here was the Pope affirming the tradition, the grace, the supreme vocation of servitude. A woman exiled from her country, her religion, her community, and even the law, having her feet cleaned by the Holy Father. It was a new way of demonstrating the oldest virtue – the divine paradox of the leader of more than a billion Catholics reminding the world that he was here to serve. This was not novelty, not trendiness, not fashion, not changing with the times, not trying to appear "relevant" but explaining to the world in the most transparent and golden manner that the Pope and his Church was at the epicentre of the body politic and body theological. The underlying tradition was continued and even extended and magnified, but the cosmetics were slightly changed.

Mark Davies is the Bishop of Shrewsbury in Britain and is one of that country's most dynamic Catholic leaders. He had fascinating things to say about all this in the May of 2013, when he addressed the Union of Catholic Mothers. The Bishop said that Pope Francis had become "the focus of fascination" in the press because of three factors: his "evident goodness," his "informal style," and his "Christian simplicity." Because of this, he continued, the media assume that all sorts of changes and reforms will shortly take place. That, he said, was certainly not the case. The Holy Father "leads us not towards abandoning the demands of the faith, as some commentators might hope or suppose, but directly to those demands in their most radical, beautiful and uncompromising essence. I can't remember how many times I have been asked, everywhere from radio stations to petrol stations, whether I liked the new Pope. To the Catholic mind this is a strange question as the loyalty we owe to the Pope is not based upon personal 'likes' or 'dislikes.' My invariable reply is that 'We love the Pope whoever he is.' This may seem just as puzzling to my questioners. Those long experienced in the media warn of something we may already see taking shape and will require of us the very supernatural perspective Pope Francis urges. They tell of how a public personality can be built up in the media. In this case, it is based on the Pope's evident good-ness and an informal style which is then contrasted even with his most saintly predecessors. Expectations are subtly or less subtly raised that this is the man who will change the Catholic faith itself in accordance with the commentator's own wishes and agenda. I noticed only last week a concern being expressed in our national media that our Holy Father is proving as 'hard-line' as his predecessors. We know, as Catholics, that the loyalty we owe to the Pope is greater than the passing loyalties people give to political figures or celebrity personalities." A roaringly direct and disarming explanation and analysis of Catholic obligations and beliefs, and media and public misunderstanding and confusion.

Something has to be stressed at this point. We do not become Catholics so as to be loved, we become Catholics so as to love. If Catholics want the first, they have almost certainly come to the wrong place. To be genuinely counter-cultural is a dangerous place to be, and Catholicism is always counter-cultural. Being loved is actually relatively easy, whereas loving is often extremely difficult. Television hosts who make politically correct noises are loved, compromising semi-Christians who travel the road of contemporary sexual ethics are loved – firm, resolute Catholics far less so, and sometimes are positively hated. This is crucial to a discussion of the future Church and the challenges that will be faced by Catholics in the coming years.

Being loved, however, is not the same as being relevant. We are often told that Catholicism is not relevant, being a prerequisite for the demand that it changes. This is sloppy reasoning. The Church is more relevant than ever, in that it's often the sole voice crying out for genuine justice, but it's less loved than it might be precisely because of its acute relevance. A small but telling case in point: Have you noticed that whenever Hollywood brings out yet another movie about the devil, the man standing up to old Nick and giving Satan a kick between the horns is never – with the greatest respect – a United Methodist minister, never a Unitarian, never even an Episcopalian!

No, it's always a Roman Catholic priest. So, when the going gets tough, the toughs get Catholic. That heroic priest defying Lucifer and all of his works is seldom lovable, but he's always relevant. Boy, is he relevant. This, of course, is the same

Hollywood that routinely marginalizes, mocks, and even abuses Catholicism and its clergy and followers in its movies – those, at least, don't mention the devil at all.

Many of the people most critical of the Church and most vociferous in demanding change and a different future play the moral prince in public while living as ethical paupers in private. It's more than mere hypocrisy and directs us to a malfunction, an arrogant presumption, at the very heart of demands for Church change. The fiercest critics insist on change because they are convinced of their own righteousness, but refuse to question whether their moral certainties are anything more than projections of their own desires and insecurities. They claim to be looking down on Catholicism from the intellectual high ground, yet more often are looking up to something they cannot understand and have no intentions of trying to do so. As I said earlier, when critics or even occasional friends of the Church call for change, they are seldom speaking of theological reforms. Actually, theology doesn't play a major role, perhaps not any genuine role at all, in the general attack on Catholicism. Theologians might regret and dispute this – well, they would, wouldn't they – but it's an absolute, I'm afraid. It's perhaps regrettable, but certainly undeniable, that very few people are rushing to the morning newspaper to find out the latest pronouncement from a theologian. "Have you seen the evening news, dear?" "Yes, amazing stuff. An obscure German theologian has demanded a rethink of Thomas Aquinas's early writings!" No, it is not theology itself that people want changed but the moral, ethical, social, and personal consequences of Catholic theology: specifically, where Church teaching affects their own lives, which frequently concerns issues of divorce, sex, and birth control. Indeed, "invariably" might be more apposite than "frequently," and in some cases "exclusively" will do the job rather well. So it's generally not the virgin birth, the immaculate conception, or transubstantiation, but condoms, remarriage, and your gay son being able to marry his partner that cause concern. Which is fair enough, I suppose, and in some ways entirely understandable, but please be honest about it.

So, whether we like it or not, many of these issues will have to be addressed in this book. And I make no apology for doing so, because they matter very much in themselves, and in particular to those who are struggling with them, often in great emotional pain. But they can be understood in Catholic terms only in the context of understanding what the Church teaches and believes. It would be far easier to write pages about predictions of numbers and growth statistics in all the various Catholic regions, or to tell the Church how it should behave, but I find both approaches, or to avoid topics that will attract criticism and enemies, but life is too short to run from conflict. Remember, we become Catholic to love, not to be loved.

Which leads us to where the Church cannot change. Not *must not* change, but *cannot* change. If readers are looking for a guidebook to Church transformation, they have come to the wrong place. Much of what follows will outline not only where there will be no alteration in Catholic teaching, but also explains why the Church believes these things, where they come from, and how this is far, far more than a matter of politics or conservatism or anything so flimsy and transitory as a new response to a new problem. Problems might appear new, but they're generally timeless dilemmas in a different wrapping paper. So the essence of the book is not the nature of change, but the nature of the future Church. I will certainly discuss how evangelization, communication, the response to abuse issues, and worship will likely change in the coming years, but I am not going to spin tales simply to satisfy doubters. The book is called *The Future of Catholicism*, not *How to Make Failed Catholics Feel Good About Themselves*, or *A Handbook for Catholics Who Want a More Protestant Church*. Oh dear, even less love now coming in my direction.

A mere two days after he was elected pontiff, Pope Francis told the Cardinal Electors gathered in Rome, "If we do not profess Jesus Christ, things go wrong. We may become a charitable NGO, but not the Church, the Bride of the Lord. When we do not profess Jesus Christ, we profess the worldliness of the devil, a demonic worldliness." This is central, absolute, essential, and inescapable. The Church does not exist to change the faith to reflect the world but to change the world to reflect the faith. Similarly, it demands that our relationship with Jesus Christ – known in completion exclusively through membership of and participation in the Catholic Church – must lead us to become more like Him, not Him more like us. Nobody ever said it would be easy being a Catholic, they said it would be right. Myriad children have wished their parents would change, but there comes a point when those kids are so grateful that Mum and Dad didn't. You know that because you were once a child, and you know that even more if you're a parent. You know it most of all if you're a serious, devout, content Catholic.

We also need to establish some of the quasi-technical points about change, future, dogma, doctrine, and teaching. These are mere words, and they are supposed to help us to understand theology and Catholicism. Tragically, theologians sometimes use them to try to make themselves sound more intelligent than they are and to cloud rather than clarify faith and religion. The admirable Catholic Answers organization once responded to a letter asking about infallibility and whether the Church of the future could be different. The letter writer had heard a priest explain that the Church had indeed changed its views many times over the centuries, and that the words of Jesus in the Gospel of Matthew – "Whatever you bind on earth shall be bound in heaven, and whatever you loose on earth shall be loosed in heaven. Again, I say to you, if two of you agree on earth about anything for which they are to pray, it shall be granted them by my heavenly Father" – gave the Church total authority to alter all sorts of teachings. The response is worth quoting at some length, because it explains a great deal of the groundwork for what is to come.

"No, the Church cannot change its doctrines no matter how badly some theologians may want it to or how loudly they claim it can. The doctrines of the Catholic Church are the deposit of faith revealed by Jesus Christ, taught by the apostles, and handed down in their entirety by the apostles to their successors. Since revealed truth cannot change, and since the deposit of faith is comprised of revealed truth, expressed in Scripture and Sacred Tradition, the deposit of faith cannot change. While it's certainly true that our Lord's words to the apostles in Matthew 18:18–19 grant authority to the apostles to 'bind' the members of the Church to believe the doctrines of the Church ('He who listens to you listens to me. He who rejects you rejects me and the one who sent me' [Lk 10:16]), the 'loosing' spoken of in Mathew 18:18 does not mean the apostles can modify doctrine. The Church does not have the power to do the impossible, to change or delete divinely revealed truth which forms the deposit of faith. Rather, the concept of loosing, as it pertains to the apostles and their successors, has more to do with the Church's ability to dispense individuals or the whole Church from observing certain ecclesiastical disciplines. There are many examples of this authority to bind and loose in the arena of Church discipline."

The site then provides some examples. Early Catholicism allowed married men to be ordained as priests in the Western church, but this was changed in the tenth century. It was once forbidden to eat meat on Fridays but that ruling has now been modified. Before Vatican II Catholics were obliged to fast from food and water from midnight until the time they received Communion. That was changed to a three-hour fast to what is now a one-hour fast. Catholic Answers continues:

"Matthew 18 also refers to the Church's authority to bind and loose with regard to sin. Every priest has the authority of Christ to 'loose' (absolve) penitents from their sins through the sacrament of confession (Jn 20:21–22, 2 Cor 5:18–20). The priest also has the obligation, in rare cases when he sees no evidence of contrition or an unwillingness on the part of the penitent to stop committing sin, to 'bind' someone in their sins by refusing to grant him absolution until he evinces genuine contrition. The faithful may gain indulgences through corporal and spiritual acts of charity, certain prayers, and pilgrimages, and are thus, by the authority of the Church's power to bind and loose, able to receive partial or complete remission of all temporal punishment due to sin. Through indulgences the Church may loose Christians from the duty of penance which would otherwise need to be performed. Certain forms of excommunication may be 'loosed' only by a bishop or, in graver circumstances, only by the Holy See. Priests and religious who request it can be 'loosed' (dispensed) from their vows of celibacy (and, in the case of religious, the vows of poverty and obedience). None of these issues deals with doctrine as such (since doctrine is unchangeable) but with Church discipline, government, and penance."[1]

This won't satisfy those who worship change rather than God, but then the god of change is an unforgiving, harsh, and relentless deity. Of course he is – he demands novelty and newness, and so can never be satisfied. The same applies to his flock. Remember, also, that those who pray for change are from the right as well as from the left. Catholic author and scholar George Weigel put it rather well when he wrote the following in an article about his book entitled *Evangelical Catholicism*[2]: "Hans Kung, out there on the far left fringes of Catholicism, has ideas about the reform of the Catholic Church; so does Bernard Fellay, the schismatic bishop and leader of the hard-right Lefebvrists. . . . Calls for Catholic reform are ubiquitous, across the landscape of Catholic opinion. But how often do we stop and think about what distinguishes authentic Catholic reform from ersatz Catholic reform? Are there criteria that help us understand what's true and false, in this matter of Catholic reform?"

It's a rhetorical question, and yes, there most certainly are such criteria. Scripture, the Papacy, the Magisterium, the deposit of faith, the historical teaching of the Church, the Church councils, the life and example of Christ Jesus. I will explain in the book how these underpinning reference points are crucial to Catholic understanding and to any possible reforms or lack of the same. We can train a human body to strengthen a limb or increase its stamina, but we cannot train a body to grow a new limb or suddenly be able to fly. The Church can change within its own context and teaching, but cannot adapt into something that it is not. It is either Catholic or it is non-Catholic or anti-Catholic; there is no middle way, and there wasn't supposed to be.

I have chosen to look at the future of Catholicism by responding to the most common questions asked about that future, and anybody who has spent time explaining or defending the Church, or reading Catholic and secular articles about it, knows exactly what those questions always are. I have devoted a chapter, an extended essay, to the key themes of same-sex marriage, abortion and contraception, euthanasia, female ordination, the refusal of communion to politicians who support and lead anti-Catholic policies and legislation and the nature of the separation of church and state, papal authority, ecumenism and the new evangelization, and a final chapter dealing with various smaller but still deeply significant issues such as the new movements within the Church, Catholicism's relationship with the developing world, the future of the Latin Mass, demographics, the detritus of the abuse scandal, and so on. These are by no means the only factors shaping the future of Catholicism, but I assure you that they are by far the most divisive, vital, and influential and challenging. In conclusion, while as a Catholic I read and love Scripture, I do not, alas, have a gift of prophecy, and this is merely one Catholic man's opinion, but it is an opinion based on Catholic teaching and extensive study, unlike the predictions and demands of the majority of journalists and writers who assume they understand God's Holy Church when in fact they have hardly even made the effort to do so.

I have not written this book to satisfy whim, but to explain permanent things, sacred things, Catholic things to a world aroused by change to a degree bordering on the pornographic and the tumescent. To a certain extent, this is the third of a series of books that began with *Why Catholics Are Right* and continued with *Heresy: Ten Lies They Spread About Christianity*, but this volume also stands alone and should certainly be read as a separate work. After Pope Francis there will be another Pope, the 267th, and after him another – assuming, that is, that the world still exists. Each time there is a conclave the same questions will be asked and the same types of people will register their incredulity, shock, horror, and contrived disappointment that the new Pope does not de-Catholicize the Church. So this book will stand the time, which is good both for me and for the book, but sad in that it means that nothing changes under the anti-Catholic sun. I am sometimes addressed by critics at my speeches who explain to me that they have a new criticism of Catholicism and a new attack on the Catholic Church. I always respond that they haven't. Not that I can read minds or doubt their intelligence, but that I have heard every anti-Catholic argument, every criticism, there is. The future of Catholicism is not especially new or different, because it is a next step, or a new stitch in a seamless cloak of truth, and is exciting in the way that only truth can be.

Because the Catholic Church is so immensely, intensely exciting, I made the conscious choice to join its ranks in 1985, as a man in his mid-twenties. I left my country, Britain, for Canada a year later because I fell in love with a Canadian woman I had met at a conference at the University of Toronto, devoted to the English Catholic author and journalist Gilbert Keith Chesterton. He brought us together, and in tribute to him we named our first son Gilbert; well, his middle name at least – it would have been cruel to saddle him with Gilbert merely to satisfy parental romanticism! Chesterton himself was once asked why he was a Catholic, and he wrote this: "There are ten thousand reasons all amounting to one reason: that Catholicism is true. I could fill all my space with separate sentences each beginning with the words, 'It is the only thing that . . .' As, for instance, (1) It is the only thing that really prevents a sin from being a secret. (2) It is the only thing in which the superior cannot be superior; in the sense of supercilious. (3) It is the only thing that frees a man from the degrading slavery of being a child of his age. (4) It is the only thing that talks as if it were the truth; as if it were a real messenger refusing to tamper with a real message. (5) It is the only type of Christianity that really contains every type of man; even the respectable man. (6) It is the only large attempt to change the world from the inside; working through wills and not laws; and so on."

That was in 1926. The same holds true almost ninety years later, and will remain true as the future of Catholicism unfolds and makes the world a brighter, lighter place.

I

MARRIAGE

IN SOME WAYS when we consider the future of Catholicism, this subject is the most central and intense question surrounding the Church's social and moral teaching, which is why this chapter is relatively long. While Catholics in the coming years will continue to hold, for example, to a strong defence of the unborn and an opposition to artificial birth control and euthanasia, these will seldom bring them into direct conflict with the state and the law, other than in relation to their work in the medical profession, their rights to protest, or with some of the more intolerant quasi-legal and censorship creations of our increasingly misnamed liberal society. In other words, it will in the future be possible to be a serious Catholic and behave accordingly regarding these issues and generally not suffer too many direct, damaging consequences. With the same-sex marriage issue and the greater, wider phenomenon of homosexuality and its various ripples – transgendered, transsexual, twin-spirited, and an ever-expanding variety of sexual categories and sub-categories – support for the gay community is now so deep and will become ever more so due to generational changes in cultural assumptions, that Catholics will find themselves at loggerheads not only with Western society's pre-set position but also with the legal process, employers, adoption agencies, schools and universities, and even the police. It's going to be an extremely tense situation for the future Church, and the pressure on that Church to change its teachings will be even stronger and more forceful than it is now. As it stands, the situation is harsh and threatening, and support for same-sex marriage has become one of the central litmus tests for social acceptability and inclusion in the body politic and polite society. In several Western countries, a declared opposition to same-sex marriage, no matter how formed that opposition might be in loving and intelligent Catholic teaching, would make it almost impossible for someone to become a prime minister or a premier, and this intolerance is finding its way into myriad aspects of our daily lives. The Catholic Church cannot and will not change its teaching on the subject, and it's vital to understand why that is. Life would be so much easier if the position could suddenly be reversed, but Catholicism, and indeed this book, is not about ease and comfort; nor – and this is imperative – has it anything to do with bigotry or prejudice, which are of course sinful and anti-Catholic, and the Church is no more going to change its teaching on condemning bigotry and prejudice than it is going to change its teaching concerning sexuality and the nature of marriage.

This cries out to be the first chapter, then, because it's the most challenging question Catholicism and Catholics will be asked and is the area where demands for change will be the strongest. How can an allegedly compassionate and loving institution, runs the theme, not allow people who genuinely love each other to celebrate and commemorate their commitment as would couples of different genders? It's not really as complex and difficult a question to answer as some people think, it's just that to be on the "wrong" side of this great debate is perhaps the last unpardonable sin of modern secularist theology. But in a way the question itself is misleading. It's not why the Catholic Church opposes same-sex marriage, but why the Catholic Church defends the Sacrament of marriage. And to explain the Church's position, and outline why this can never change and why the future Church will always proclaim marriage as being the union of one man and one woman, we have to spend some time discussing the Catholic understanding of sexuality, sex, human dignity, and natural law. Let's state immediately, however, that the Church can, and in various countries has, accepted civil unions: that is, the legal recognition of same-sex couples as having a particular and special bond, one that is recognized officially within the constitutional and social framework of a nation-state, and accepted as meaningful by others in that society. Sadly, even where Catholic leaders have accepted civil unions, this has done little to dilute attacks on Catholicism as being anti-gay and has not prevented subsequent campaigns for full same-sex marriage. That was the case, for example, in the United Kingdom, where civil unions were seen not as a compromise but as the first step to complete acceptance of same-sex marriage. It's what many Catholics predicted would happen when they originally opposed civil unions in Britain.

But let's begin with the premise that a Catholic defence of traditional marriage and opposition to same-sex marriage is now and in the future certainly will be a point of persecution for Catholics, both at a personal and organizational level. This stance is not going to change under the new Pope or any other. In fact, Pope Francis found himself in direct and fierce conflict with the Argentinian government in 2010 when he opposed its same-sex marriage legislation. "What is at stake," he said, "is the identity and survival of the family: father, mother, and children. What is at stake are the lives of so many children who are discriminated against in advance, deprived of the human maturation that God wanted to give them with a father and a mother. What is at stake is a direct rejection of God's law, which is also engraved in our hearts. Let's not be naïve: it is not just a political struggle; it is a destructive claim against God's plan. It is not merely a legislative bill (this is only the instrument) but a move by the Father of Lies who seeks to confuse and deceive the children of God." It's difficult to imagine how he could have been more direct and clear in his and the Church's position. He described the bill to introduce same-sex marriage and institute gay adoption as follows: "The bill will be discussed in the Senate after July 13. Look at San Jose, Maria, Child and ask them [to] fervently defend Argentina's family at this time. [Be reminded] what God told his people in a time of great anguish: 'This war is not yours but God's.' May they succor, defend and join God in this war." His comment that gay adoption represented a form of "discrimination against children" even led Argentine president Cristina Fernández de Kirchner to respond that the remarks suggested "medieval times and the Inquisition." She may have been guilty of irresponsible hyperbole, but she was speaking for more people than we might like to believe. But the Pope was speaking Catholic truth to secular power, for the current and future Church.

Truth can, indeed, land people in all sorts of trouble. In the United States, Catholic activist and author Maggie Gallagher is a leading and outspoken campaigner for traditional marriage. In August 2012, a gunman entered the Washington, D.C., offices of the pro-traditional marriage Family Research Council (FRC) and shot a guard and attempted to attack people working there. He was heavily armed. Gallagher wrote a column shortly after the incident: "The FRC shooting came a week after a package addressed to me personally showed up in the National Organization for Marriage offices filled with feces and hate and used condoms. The police LGBT hate crimes division was called to the scene . . . and told the cops not to investigate it as a hate crime. In at least two instances, to my direct knowledge, a crime directed at a person or organization who opposes gay marriage was not investigated by D.C. cops as a bias crime," she wrote. "A nasty package is a minor event. A shooter who intended mass murder is deadly serious. Together they make up a pattern." It's standard practice now. The bully and the abuser escape, because the increasingly prevalent view is that the Catholic Church's opposition to same-sex marriage moves beyond normal and usual behaviour, bleeding into a grey area of law and policing. This also applies to politics. Catholic politician and former Republican senator Rick Santorum is a strong opponent of same-sex marriage but also a highly considerate and compassionate man who has been careful to support marriage while not attacking gay people. He has spoken and written on the theme many times, and his views are far from hateful.

"I think that's the foundational flaw with this whole debate. The law is as it has been for 200-plus years, and so the burden is on them to make the persuasive case as to why they should be married, not just for their benefit but for what the impact is on society and marriage as a whole, and on children. I would argue that the gay community has not made the argument. They may have made the argument as to why they want it, but they have not made any arguments as to why this is beneficial for society. They have not made any argument – convincing or otherwise, that I'm aware of – as to what the impact would be on heterosexual marriages and what the impact would be on children. They have no studies. They have no information whatsoever about what it would do to the moral ecology of the country, what it would do to religious liberty, what it would do to the mental and physical health of children – nothing. They've made no case. Basically the case they've made is, 'We want what you want, and therefore you should give it to us,'" he explained in a Pew Forum interview in 2008. You might not agree with him, but it's not exactly a call for genocide!

"What I've noticed about this debate is that fewer and fewer people are stepping up and taking the position I'm taking because they see the consequences of doing so. I don't think there is an issue that is a tougher issue for people to stand up against in American culture today than this one, both from the standpoint of the mainstream media and the popular culture condemning you for your – they can use all sorts of words to describe you – intolerant, bigot, homophobe, hater. The other side takes it personally. And so it makes it very difficult for folks to stand up and argue public policy when the other side views it as a personal, direct assault on them. So it's very, very hard for me to be optimistic when we have a battle of ideas and one side is universally hammered for being intolerant bigots and the other side is enlightened and tolerant – which I think is false, but it is the pervasive attitude. We know that the American public doesn't approve of same-sex marriage, but they are uncomfortable about it because, again, the public perception is if you feel that way, you're a bigot or a hater. And if the culture continues to send that message, if our educational system sends that message, which it does, you know, eventually the culture will change and people's opinions will change. The push back is what most people know: that mothers and fathers bring some-thing unique. I mean, I have six children."

Quite so, and the lines of "dialogue" were already well marked. In May 2003, gay activist Dan Savage was so outraged that the Roman Catholic Santorum opposed same-sex marriage that he asked his readers in his highly influential syndicated columns and website to make up a new, insulting definition for the man's surname. "There's no better way to memorialize the Santorum scandal," suggested the inexorably angry and cruel Savage, "than by attaching his name to a sex act that would make his big, white teeth fall out of his big, empty head." The chosen name, and God only knows how the sick man picked his lucky winner, was "the frothy mixture of lube and fecal matter that is sometimes the by-product of anal sex." Savage then created entire new websites, called spreadingsantorum.com and santorum.com, and did all he could to promote the new definition on the Internet and told his followers to spread the abuse. It worked. So much so that Santorum, a father of children old enough to also be victimized by this, asked Google to remove the new definition, but Google steadfastly refused to do so. In 2010, Savage offered to take down his sites himself if Santorum gave $5 million to Freedom to Marry, a group that campaigned for same-sex marriage. It was a form of blackmail, and Santorum was having none of it. The definition continues to be one of the leading, if not the leading, definition for the Santorum name on Google, Yahoo, and Bing search engines. That was the state of affairs in 2010; it has got far worse now, and every indication is that it will continue to become even more hateful and censorious.

Sometimes even the most vulnerable Catholics are hurt by the intolerance of supporters of same-sex marriage. In 2011, the Catholic Diocese of Rockford, Illinois, announced that it was closing its adoption agencies, after being forced out of service due to new legislation that would oblige them to place children in their care with homosexual couples. Catholic Charities of Illinois had spent more than a century providing adoption and foster care to countless children and at the time of closing dealt with almost four hundred children and employed more than fifty people. The organization had an exemplary record and was renowned for its compassion, dedication, and professionalism. The reason for the closure was that the state of Illinois had introduced the Religious Freedom Protection and Civil Unions Act, protecting the right of gay couples against discrimination. The Roman Catholic diocese, along with other Christian groups, asked for an amendment that would have allowed them to refer unmarried couples, whether gay or heterosexual, to other agencies so as to not violate the teachings of the Catholic Church. It seemed entirely reasonable, in that gay couples would still be able to adopt and foster, and a Catholic agency would be able to continue being Catholic and also help vulnerable children. But the spirit of intolerance triumphed again. Babies may suffer, people will lose jobs, but no gay person would ever face the possibility of being told that there was an alternative agency more suited to their needs.

"Catholic Charities and other religious agencies implored the State of Illinois to allow their agencies to refer such couples to other adoption and foster care agencies so as to not violate the moral teachings of their faith," said Penny Wiegert, diocesan director of communication. "Tragically, that did not happen. Because of this failure and the anticipated legal challenges it will present to our free exercise of religion, the Diocese of Rockford is forced to discontinue all state-funded adoption and foster care operations." Ellen B. Lynch, general counsel for the Rockford diocese, was more blunt. "Legally, albeit emotionally painful, we determined this was the right decision to make for the moral and financial future of the Diocese of Rockford. The law of our land has always guaranteed its people freedom of religion. Denying this exemption to faith-based agencies leads one to believe that our lawmakers prefer laws that guarantee freedom from religion. We simply cannot compromise the spirit that motivates us to deliver quality, professional services to families by letting our state define our religious teachings."[1]

Just as in the United States, Catholic adoption agencies and even individuals in Britain have been affected by the war on dissent waged by supporters of same-sex marriage. British-based Roman Catholic adoption agencies in particular – with more than a century of saving children from often horrendously difficult and poor backgrounds – have for some time now explained that there was a direct contradiction and conflict for them in this area, and they could not give children to gay couples, as Catholic teaching, the very teaching that led them to give so much time, money, and love to children in the first place, prevented them from doing so. In that very few if any gay couples would apply to a Catholic agency anyway, it seemed a moot point. Surely, most people and all reasonable people argued, a way could be found to accommodate both parties, because the well-being of the children was what really mattered here. Alas, it was not to be. Writing in the *Christian Science Monitor*, Sally Thompson explained: "This week the last Catholic adoption agency in the UK has been forced to cease adoptions following the ruling of the Charity Commission. Catholic Care, a Leeds-based social care organization, only offers adoption services to heterosexual married couples. The Commission has ruled that their religious views do not justify its refusal to place children with homosexual couples. Gay rights campaigners may see this result as a victory, but I believe it reflects a growing trend of trampling on religious groups' liberties and will mean young, vulnerable children will lose out. Catholic Care has been offering adoption services for over 100 years, successfully placing children with families and offering post-adoption support services. It has a much better record than a lot of adoption agencies run purely by local authorities and receives its funding from the Catholic Church. By removing the agency's right to offer adoption to heterosexual couples only, the Commission has effectively cut off funding for this service, as the Church will not give money to support a service that acts contrary to their beliefs. As a result, orphans and vulnerable children will lose out as a respected provider of these services is forced to close. It remains to be seen whether other agencies will be able to increase their provision in the area to make up for this. Secondly, although the agency chooses not to help homosexual couples adopt, it does not actively prohibit it or encourage homophobia of any sort. Catholic Care is not stopping gay people adopting, it is just refusing to be forced into helping them do so. Homosexual couples are free to adopt using other adoption service providers in the area. Lastly it's wrong that, for the sake of the government's crusade against discrimination, this quango is ending the good work Catholic Care do in the community. Their decision will bring no benefit to the local community and only continues to stoke concern over the growing limitations the government is placing on religious groups who seek to serve the community in accordance with their convictions."[2]

What she didn't mention was that, irony of ironies, Catholic Care had attempted to use a loophole that has long been used by homosexual charities. The government's Sexual Orientation Regulations was originally introduced to guarantee that gay organizations could not be sued for discrimination when they dealt exclusively with gay people. What was good enough for them, it seemed, was not good enough for those who disagreed with them. This was absolutism and triumphalism. The views of millions of Roman Catholics, the future of the children, and the beliefs of perhaps most British people, were trampled in this rush to stamp out all disagreement with same-sex marriage in any form, including people who owned small hotels or bed and breakfasts, or rented out rooms in their own homes, and continue to hold to a strong religious teaching about the nature of marriage.

In Spain, where same-sex marriage was introduced as early as 2005, following a long hearing a judge finally dropped charges against Roman Catholic Bishop Juan Antonio Reig Pla brought after the prelate had criticized the marriage decision and the gay lifestyle. The Spanish newspaper *El Pais* explained that Judge Antonio Cervera Pelaez-Campomanes dismissed the lawsuit by arguing that, "while the bishop's words indicate a critical view of homosexuality, they do not, properly understood, inflict harm on homosexuals in general nor are they are a call to discrimination on the basis of sexual orientation." But this was after a prolonged period of legal defence, enormous costs, emotional trauma, public and media attacks, and the very real threat of conviction. In some of these cases, while the defendant eventually wins, the financial burden can be so great that their lives are transformed, and they are – and this is deeply pertinent – unable to participate in any further public debate. In this example, the bishop used strong language to condemn gay marriage and homosexuality in general, but also spoke out against abortion, heterosexual adultery and promiscuity, alcoholism, the exploitation of workers by employers, and Christian hypocrisy. He made the remarks during a Good Friday sermon, and frankly they were entirely in keeping with the spirit of the occasion and his office. Even so, gay groups demanded not only that he be charged but also expelled from the city.

There are dozens of other examples, but what we need to establish at this point is why the Church teaches as it does on the issue, and how this means intrinsically that the future Church simply cannot alter its approach and beliefs. Ask any active Catholic, any priest, any bishop, and they would tell you that life would be a great deal easier and more simple if the Church could and did. But marriage is one of the Church's seven Sacraments, and as with all Catholic theology this is an extension of Biblical truths combined with the wisdom of the deposit of Catholic faith and the teaching of the Magisterium. Biblical responses can sound strong, hard, and even fierce to modern ears and sensibilities. If they give offence, I apologize, but the truth of a position cannot be obscured or disguised simply because it gives offence, and this context will shape the Church of the future, for the future. Nobody has to accept Catholic teachings, but they are nevertheless Catholic teachings. The Internet is bursting with attempted revisions and explanations by gay people, many of whom are struggling – and who can blame them? – to somehow argue away what appears to be an absolute condemnation of homosexuality in the Bible and in Catholic history. It appears that way because it is that way. Love has to inform everything that is Catholic, but Catholics do not confuse love with agreement and consent. There are moral absolutes in the Catholic faith, including and perhaps especially regarding sexuality, heterosexual as well as homosexual. But let's begin with an attack that is central because it is common, almost iconic now, and also typifies the way the Catholic attitude toward homosexuality and same-sex marriage is and will continue to be treated by the mainstream.

Welcome to Father Straw Man. Either by ignorance or concerted malice, supporters of gay marriage have constructed false and utterly untrue arguments that, runs the canard, are proposed by imaginary Catholics, and then – naturally and easily – they tear them apart. These, they argue, are the theological and Biblical positions behind the case for traditional marriage, and not only do they not stand up to scrutiny, but they are downright absurd. Well, of course that's the case, because they are not our arguments at all, any more than the radio caller reciting, "God created Adam and Eve, not Adam and Steve" is our argument. The talk-radio warrior is not a theologian, and the Catholic defence made up by a tendentious gay group or a Hollywood scriptwriter is not in any way a reflection of the complex, nuanced, kind, and highly sophisticated Catholic response to same-sex marriage and its advocates.

Fundamental to this is a long Old Testament passage that has been used numerous times and in numerous places to, frankly, make Catholics look silly. It was used on television's *The West Wing*, it was distributed to millions of people on the Internet, it's been used by television hosts and journalists, even been used by leading politicians. Best of all, perhaps, was when gay campaigner and former *Star Trek* supporting actor and *Howard Stern Show* cast member George Takei posted an illustrated version of it on his Facebook site. Well, if Helmsman Sulu says it's so, then who are we to doubt his Starfleet wisdom? Beam me up, gay activist. One of the early times the attack was employed was against Dr. Laura Schlessinger, a convert to Orthodox Judaism and a social conservative generally supportive of Catholic teaching on marriage, who allegedly said that homosexuality was an abomination according to Leviticus 18:22. In fact, Schlessinger, who was subjected to well-organized and quite brutal boycott campaigns and personal abuse by the gay movement and was eventually forced off the air on many radio stations, had a multifaceted objection to homosexuality and thus to gay marriage, and her convictions were far more complex than the mere quoting of Scripture. But the point here is not so much her stance on gay marriage as the way sacred text is twisted purposely or accidentally, to confuse people and make those who believe in it appear ridiculous or hateful. Dr. Laura, as we have said, is not a Catholic but an Orthodox Jew, but the attacks remain the same. The following is a response to Dr. Laura's Scripture-based opposition to same-sex marriage that was posted on the Internet, went viral, and has since been used more times than I have seen on television shows telling us what the "new normal" is and how only fools, haters, and Catholics oppose same-sex marriage.

"Dear Dr. Laura: Thank you for doing so much to educate people regarding God's Law. I have learned a great deal from your show, and try to share that knowledge with as many people as I can. When someone tries to defend the homosexual life-style, for example, I simply remind them that Leviticus 18:22 clearly states it to be an abomination. . . . End of debate. I do need some advice from you, however, regarding some other elements of God's Laws and how to follow them.

"1. Leviticus 25:44 states that I may possess slaves, both male and female, provided they are purchased from neighbor-ing nations. A friend of mine claims that this applies to Mexicans, but not Canadians. Can you clarify? Why can't I own Canadians? 2. I would like to sell my daughter into slavery, as sanctioned in Exodus 21:7. In this day and age, what do you think would be a fair price for her? 3. I know that I am allowed no contact with a woman while she is in her period of Menstrual uncleanliness – Lv 15:19–24. The problem is how do I tell? I have tried asking, but most women take offense. 4. When I burn a bull on the altar as a sacrifice, I know it creates a pleasing odor for the Lord – Lv 1:9. The problem is my neighbors. They claim the odor is not pleasing to them. Should I smite them? 5. I have a neighbor who insists on working on the Sabbath. Exodus 35:2 clearly states he should be put to death. Am I morally obligated to kill him myself, or should I ask the police to do it?

"6. A friend of mine feels that even though eating shellfish is an abomination, Lv 11:10, it is a lesser abomination than homosexuality. I don't agree. Can you settle this? Are there 'degrees' of abomination? 7. Lv 21:20 states that I may not approach the altar of God if I have a defect in my sight. I have to admit that I wear reading glasses. Does my vision have to be 20/20, or is there some wiggle-room here? 8. Most of my male friends get their hair trimmed, including the hair around their temples, even though this is expressly forbidden by Lv 19:27. How should they die? 9. I know from Lv 11:6–8 that touching the skin of a dead pig makes me unclean, but may I still play football if I wear gloves? 10. My uncle has a farm. He violates Lv 19:19 by planting two different crops in the same field, as does his wife by wearing garments made of two different kinds of thread (cotton/polyester blend). He also tends to curse and blaspheme a lot. Is it really necessary that we go to all the trouble of getting the whole town together to stone them? Lv 24:10–16. Couldn't we just burn them to death at a private family affair, like we do with people who sleep with their in-laws? (Lv 20:14)

"I know you have studied these things extensively and thus enjoy considerable expertise in such matters, so I'm confident you can help. Thank you again for reminding us that God's word is eternal and unchanging. Your adoring fan (It would be a damn shame if we couldn't own a Canadian)."

As a Canadian, I find this rather offensive. Seriously, however, as a Catholic and – perhaps more significantly – as a logical and thinking person, I find it downright insulting. It's Internet wisdom, paperback scholarship, entirely typical of a culture that feels rather than reflects, and reacts rather than responds. It's also incredibly arrogant and condescending, in that the writer obviously assumes all Catholics are incredibly gullible, and that after years of study, reading, prayer, and faith this banal response to what is not even the genuine Catholic position on marriage will somehow expose and destroy the Catholic argument. In some ways it's entirely typical: in spite of Cardinal Newman, Thomas Aquinas, Nicolaus Copernicus, and so on and so on, Catholics are considered stupid and slow, and the clever people are those who have bought – but perhaps not read yet but, hey, we're so busy – a book by Christopher Hitchens or Richard Dawkins. This applies not just to the marriage issue and is something the future Church will have to confront on a regular basis.

A few things have to be said immediately. The Old Testament is understood by Catholics only and essentially through the prism of the New, just as a book can only be properly and completely understood if we read it fully and reach the ending. Catholics believe that Christ came to fulfil God's plan, to give the world the denouement to the story, to tie up the loose ends, explain and clarify what was as yet not completely understood and clear. No Catholic worth the name could or should quote the Old Testament without reference to and understanding of the New Testament, and without understanding Christ's message to the world. By the way, Orthodox Jews also rely on interpretation of the books of Moses, and to dismiss centuries of rabbinical study and scholarship in a sound bite designed merely to score a political point is not only anti-intellectual but downright rude.

Catholic theologians have for millennia drawn a distinction between the moral law and the civil and ceremonial law. They had no option, because Christ Himself did so. If you have any doubts, ask why for two thousand years Catholic men have not had to be circumcised, Catholic women not had to take ritual baths, and so on. Christ emphasized the unending continuity of the moral law of the Old Testament, but simultaneously told us that the laws of custom and tribe given by Moses to a specific people and at a specific time no longer applied to God's people, who were, remember, not just the Jews now but, after the final sacrifice, that of Himself, Jesus Christ, to all of humanity. It really is basic and entirely logical stuff, if only people would think about it. But thinking about it requires, yes, thinking about it. There is nothing clever or smart – in fact, the very opposite – in writing a letter or quoting something on a television show that reveals the writer, the speaker, to be supremely ignorant of the reality of history and the vital nuances and distinctions of theology. From its earliest days, from the first century, the Catholic Church taught the strictest interpretation of the Old Testament's moral laws, but also from its earliest days, from the first century, the same Catholic Church taught that the ceremonial laws applied only to the past, to the ancient Jews, and not to the new covenant and the new religion. More than this, those Jewish followers of Jesus in the handful of years following the crucifixion and resurrection who did question whether the old, civil laws still applied were quickly and repeatedly told that they were wrong. The same Bible the supporters of same-sex marriage criticize and mock regarding a supposed inconsistency in the supplication of laws shows in the New Testament that the Catholics asking for ceremonial laws to continue into Catholic belief were roundly defeated.[3]

Morality does not change in essence, but social mores and dietary and culinary commands obviously and certainly do. It's self-evident and true, and doesn't become less so just because a famous actor says it is so on international television. This is something the future Catholic Church must stress in its defence of values and virtues that will be challenged and marginalized. If we were to be consistent about the argument about the Old Testament being unreliable, we would also have to reject the belief in a single God, in not stealing or lying, not being envious or – difficult ground here – committing adultery. So yes, Leviticus 18:22 shows that God considers homosexuality an abomination but – accusers say – it also promises punishment for those who do not keep kosher and so on. Let's look more closely. The ancient Hebrews were a people living in the desert, chosen by God to deliver a message to humanity, and thus it was essential that they survive, and to survive they had to be healthy. The dietary laws kept them apart from others, not because of their pride but because God wanted to keep them firm and independent. Other nations were considered unclean. Once they left the desert, once Jesus, a Jew, had been given to the world, those laws that do indeed today seem obscure and absurd did not apply. The laws regarding right and wrong, human dignity, the integrity of the person, and God's plan for procreation – more of this later – obviously still did. The attack is more accurately applied to Jewish people than Catholics, but it would still be inaccurate, and also considered vaguely anti-Semitic; in a society where anti-Jewish attitudes are still and rightly considered unacceptable, Catholic bashing is almost a pre-set position for the chattering classes.

The attacks on the Old Testament are also significant because they characterize the anti-intellectualism of so many of the responses to the Catholic opposition to same-sex marriage: historical anachronism, ignorance of historical context, and the assumption that religious people who do not accept same-sex marriage must be motivated by ignorance or hatred. My experience of Catholics – and while this is obviously anecdotal, it is based on widespread experience in several countries – is that they fully understand why some gay people campaign for same-sex marriage. They may be wrong, most Catholics appear to believe, but their demands are understandable. I certainly do not attribute base motives to people with whom I agree, unless they prove otherwise, and I wish there was more dialogue between informed, serious, orthodox Catholics and gay advocates. But truth be told, whenever Catholics make their position clear, the response is invariably boycott, attack, shouting down, and anger, or pure and utter caricature.

The Deuteronomy response to same-sex marriage is, in reality, seldom heard from Catholics, and never without explanation, qualification, and context. It is, as I said above, part of the straw man approach so enjoyed by gay people today when they try to defeat Catholics in argument or just make them appear ridiculous. It's difficult to express how enervating it is to see skilled actors on television, on stage, and in movies, often attractive and appealing people, deliver the standard Old Testament line in portentous tones, usually to smiling, approving colleagues, or to a group of other actors playing dumb and dumbfounded Catholics who, God knows how, have no intelligent response and clearly know nothing about their Bible. Have you noticed how these fictitious opponents of same-sex marriage on the screen suddenly know nothing about the Bible they've just quoted and apparently read all of the time, but the fictitious supporters of same-sex marriage who don't even believe in the thing are suddenly veritable Biblical scholars? In some ways it's very funny, but also horrendous emotional bullying and profoundly misleading.

Nor is this the only Old Testament reference to homosexuality. As early as Genesis 19, two angels in disguise visit the city of Sodom and are offered shelter by Lot. That evening, the Sodomites – yes, it's difficult to not laugh – demand that Lot allow his guests to be given to them so that they can have sexual intercourse with them. Lot even offers his daughters instead of his male guests, but the locals have, well, specific tastes. Lot protects the angels, who then blind their attackers. Lot and his people escape, and Sodom is destroyed by God. The understanding and interpretation of the text is obvious: God punished Sodom due to its homosexuality, and the word itself subsequently became a byword for homosexuality. This understanding of the text wasn't seriously questioned until the later twentieth century, when gay commentators, in an effort to reconcile the Bible with homosexuality, suggested that Sodom's crime was one of inhospitality rather than homosexuality. Which must make every manager of a busy and understaffed hotel extremely worried! You have to admire the effort behind this revision, but it's a challenge to take it seriously. There are several references in the Bible to people being inhospitable, and they are not punished at all, let alone blinded and killed. But every reference to homosexuality in Scripture is greeted with extreme retribution. Indeed Scripture is self-supporting and self-justifying, in that Jude 7 states that Sodom and Gomorrah "acted immorally and indulged in unnatural lust." The book of Ezekiel certainly does mention Sodom's lack of hospitality, but emphasizes the "abominable thing" that the town was punished for – remember, Leviticus described homosexual activity as "an abomination," and the word is not repeated elsewhere by accident.[4]

The New Testament presents even greater problems for proponents of same-sex marriage and those who would have us believe that the Bible does not oppose homosexual behaviour. Paul's Letters to the Romans is considered by many scholars to be the man's masterpiece, the centre of his theology, and one of the most important founding documents of Christianity. In the first few passages, it refers to humanity's failings and lists unacceptable actions and behaviours, and sins, that are displeasing to God. Translations vary, but the New International Version is pretty standard, and this passage is worth quoting in full:

"The wrath of God is being revealed from heaven against all the godlessness and wickedness of people, who suppress the truth by their wickedness, since what may be known about God is plain to them, because God has made it plain to them. For since the creation of the world God's invisible qualities – his eternal power and divine nature – have been clearly seen, being understood from what has been made, so that people are without excuse. For although they knew God, they neither glorified him as God nor gave thanks to him, but their thinking became futile and their foolish hearts were darkened. Although they claimed to be wise, they became fools and exchanged the glory of the immortal God for images made to look like a mortal human being and birds and animals and reptiles. Therefore God gave them over in the sinful desires of their hearts to sexual impurity for the degrading of their bodies with one another. They exchanged the truth about God for a lie, and worshiped and served created things rather than the Creator – who is forever praised. Amen.

"Because of this, God gave them over to shameful lusts. Even their women exchanged natural sexual relations for unnatural ones. In the same way the men also abandoned natural relations with women and were inflamed with lust for one another. Men committed shameful acts with other men, and received in themselves the due penalty for their error.

Furthermore, just as they did not think it worthwhile to retain the knowledge of God, so God gave them over to a depraved mind, so that they do what ought not to be done. They have become filled with every kind of wickedness, evil, greed and depravity. They are full of envy, murder, strife, deceit and malice. They are gossips, slanderers, God-haters, insolent, arrogant and boastful; they invent ways of doing evil; they disobey their parents; they have no understanding, no fidelity, no love, no mercy. Although they know God's righteous decree that those who do such things deserve death, they not only continue to do these very things but also approve of those who practice them."[5]

Extremely strong stuff, and not leaving very much if any room for ambiguity. Paul also repeats that homosexuality is one of the sins that prevents people from reaching heaven. In 1 Corinthians he says: "Do you not know that the wicked will not inherit the kingdom of God? Do not be deceived: Neither the sexually immoral nor idolaters nor adulterers nor male prostitutes nor homosexual offenders nor thieves nor the greedy nor drunkards nor slanderers nor swindlers will inherit the kingdom of God." I can only imagine how painful this is for gay people to read, but it is what it is. Any search on Amazon or Google will reveal book after book written to explain why all of this is untrue and misunderstood, and books explaining the obvious are somehow pushed much further down the list or even obscured entirely. But the word no said a thousand times will not change the answer if it is yes.

Defenders of homosexuality and gay marriage respond to Paul's writings by arguing that they need a modern translation and a contemporary interpretation, that Paul was a prisoner of his time, that he was captured by ancient ignorance and prejudice, that we need a new, more open-minded understanding of how ancient texts apply to contemporary morals, and that homo-sexuality is not in fact explicitly mentioned in the four Gospels themselves. We hear this a great deal today, and it will be applied increasingly in the future: the notion that as we learn more about homosexuality, we will come to understand that Catholic teaching is based on a false premise and thus has to change. If this argument is accepted – and there are more than a few Catholics who dearly want to compromise on this debate – there is nothing stopping a future Church being forced to compromise on any number of its moral teachings. Dangerous, dangerous thinking. As Romano Penna, professor of New Testament studies at the Pontifical Lateran University in Rome and one of the most respected scholars on this issue in the world, says:

"The writings of the New Testament do not deal explicitly with the subject of homosexuality. There are references to it, but these are quite rare, all being limited to the Pauline Epistles. The most logical explanation for this fact lies not in a permissive attitude towards the matter, but in the fact that homosexuality had already been condemned by Jewish tradition, to which all the early Christian writers are basically indebted, and that similarly in the Greek world it was censured by the predominant Stoic philosophy as contrary to nature. Thus, in the context of the first century, Philo of Alexandria, who is the leading exponent of Hellenistic Judaism, in his treatises repeatedly criticizes sodomy and pederasty as 'illicit relations' (On Abraham 135) and those that practice them as 'enemies of nature' (Special Laws 3:36); in the same way the Stoic philosopher Musonius Rufus defines homosexuality as 'against nature' (Diatribe 12), while the Roman historian Tacitus speaks openly of the 'degeneration of youth' with reference to its practice during the time of Nero (Annals 14, 20, 4). The New Testament therefore did not have any particular battle to fight on this front, needing only to align itself with the positions current in the cultural world of the first century. What was new, if anything, as invariably happens in an ethical discussion, were the reasons given for urging its avoidance."[6]

In other words, we do not need to affirm what has already been routinely and self-evidently affirmed, or deny what is already universally denied.

Paul's condemnation of male and female homosexuality simultaneously is rare in the ancient world. It's rare, in fact, in many other contexts and eras as well. Islam has different and specific penalties for male and female homosexuality, Queen Victoria refused to believe lesbianism even existed, and the National Socialists targeted homosexual men, particularly if they were effeminate and Jewish and socialist as well, but did not arrest and incarcerate lesbians – perhaps the first time Islam, Queen Victoria, and Nazism have ever been juxtaposed. In ancient times there are two other examples of such a critique of homosexuality, in Plato's writing (Laws I, 636c) and in a first-century Hellenized Jewish poetic treatise usually attributed to a Pseudo-Phocilides (Sentences 191–192). Paul, however, is different and new. He is discussing what he sees as the immorality that is a consequence of not knowing or of rejecting God. Homosexuality, he insists, is not the only sin but part of an entire package of vices that infect the pagan or the atheist. It's important to get the emphasis and the balance right here, and the same applies to the overall Christian approach to homosexuality. There are two errors into which people can fall. The first is to pretend that Scripture – be it the Old Testament, or Christ Himself – does not condemn homosexuality at all. The second is to be obsessed about, concentrate on, one particular aspect of Christian belief and to devote an unhealthy amount of time and effort to one aspect of an all-embracing way of life and belief. Sadly, the latter is what characterizes and unifies the Christian who has rather lost his way, and the former the gay activist who lost his some time ago. Paul does not single out homosexuality for censure, but neither does he pretend it is acceptable.

But, it is argued, Paul as well as most of the authors of the Bible were unaware of the nuances and complexities of homosexuality and didn't appreciate the love that people of the same gender could have for one another. The ancients and the early Christians, runs the argument, confused genuine affection and commitment between two people of the same gender with simple and vulgar lust. Problem is, this is a suburban and unsophisticated view of the ancient world, is ironically anachronistic in itself, is ahistorical and simply wrong. The authors of Scripture and the early Christians in general may have used a different language and obviously didn't use the modern quasi-scientific vocabulary that is used, often over-used, today, but they were very much aware of the many and various forms of homosexuality that existed and were perhaps more familiar with homosexuality than most people today. While the Jews rejected and condemned homosexual relationships, there were numerous ancient, pagan cultures that allowed and even celebrated homoeroticism and homosexual partnerships. Christianity, however, insists that we acknowledge the brokenness of humanity, not just of individual humans, and offers as the divine solution, the Godly fix, a faith in Jesus Christ. For the Christian, from Paul two thousand years ago to Catholic followers of Christ today, the way to deal with sexual temptation is not to pretend that it is no longer sinful, but to ask God for help to lead and live a different and transformed life. Perhaps not a heterosexual life, but a celibate life. Paul was as aware of what homosexuality was as we are today, and perhaps even more so; the Catholic Church, now and in the future, will argue that the fact that some of us have changed our attitude toward homosexuality says more about our lack of faith than about Paul's lack of knowledge and sophistication. Catholics consider rejection of God and of His plans for us as a form of rebellion. They consider that one of God's first and primary commands was that we should go forth and multiply, that man and woman should join in loving union and continue the human race, and that the rejection of this possibility through homosexuality is one of the earliest forms of rebellion against God. It may anger some modern sensibilities, but it is nevertheless the Catholic point of view. One, by the way, that is increasingly placing Catholicism in opposition to the modern psyche and culture, leading to repeated clashes and disagreements; a key component, as I say, of the relationship between the future Church and the culture around it.

Another approach to the subject from supporters of same-sex marriage, another attempt to dismantle what really is an essential and intrinsic aspect of Christianity, is based on translation and interpretation, and the argument that Paul was not referring to homosexuality at all, but to some form of shrine prostitution or to child abuse or pedophilia. These actions would, of course, be condemned by almost everybody today. This argument is, though, the apotheosis of wishful thinking. There are two specific words that some have tried to dispute: *malakoi* and *arsenokoitai*. The word *arsenokoitai* is fascinating because it is unique to Paul, and a compound from the older Greek Leviticus word describing "those who lie with a male as with a female." The exact meaning of malakoi is "soft ones" and is usually applied to sexual indulgence and licence in general but in particular to the passive member of a homosexual couple. Used together, there is no doubt to what they refer and to what Paul was trying to say. Any possible link to young boys being used by older men in the temple is exceedingly odd, linguistically and historically unsupportable, and clearly inaccurate and a modern leap of faith rather than an act of reason. None – not some, not a few, but none – of those Christian thinkers and leaders who followed Paul and who knew him and his views and writing style thought he was referring to anything other than adult and consenting homosexuality.

Robert Gagnon, author of the crucial and seminal book *The Bible and Homosexual Practice: Texts and Hermeneutics*, writes, "Ancient Israel, early Judaism and early Christianity never adopted the position that they should alter their ethical standards simply because the broader cultural milieu took a more accepting view of some practices. They all lived in environments where male-male intercourse was often more of an accepted practice than it is in our own contemporary culture. Yet, far from capitulating on their position regarding acceptable sexual expression, they maintained clear distinctions between their own practices and the practices of those outside the community of God. This is what holiness refers to: being set apart for the exclusive use of God rather than conforming to the ways of the world. Jesus himself called on his followers to be 'the light of the world' and 'a city built on a hill,' and not to act 'like the Gentiles.' The view of Scripture against same-sex intercourse is pervasive, absolute and strong, and was all those things in relation to the broader cultural contexts from which Scripture emerged. It was then, and remains today, a core countercultural vision for human sexuality."[7]

But let's take a closer look at what Jesus Himself actually said. Robert Gagnon again, this time responding to the allegation that Jesus says nothing explicit about the issue, and thus that it could not have mattered to Him. "There is no historical basis for arguing that Jesus might have been neutral or even favorable toward same-sex intercourse. All the evidence we have points overwhelmingly to the conclusion that Jesus would have strongly opposed same-sex intercourse had such behavior been a serious problem among first-century Jews. It simply was not a problem in Israel. First, Jesus' alleged silence has to be set against the backdrop of unequivocal and strong opposition to same-sex intercourse in the Hebrew Bible and throughout early Judaism. It is not historically likely that Jesus overturned any prohibition of the Mosaic law, let alone on a strongly held moral matter such as this. And Jesus was not shy about disagreeing with prevailing viewpoints. Had he wanted his disciples to take a different viewpoint he would have had to say so. Second, the notion of Jesus' 'silence' has to be qualified. According to Mark, Jesus spoke out against porneia, 'sexual immorality' (Mark 7:21–23) and accepted the Decalogue commandment against adultery (Mark 10:19). In Jesus' day, and for many centuries before and thereafter, porneia was universally understood in Judaism to include same-sex intercourse. Moreover, the Decalogue commandment against adultery was treated as a broad rubric prohibiting all forms of sexual practice that deviated from the creation model in Genesis 1–2, including homoerotic intercourse.

"It is time to deconstruct the myth of a sexually tolerant Jesus. Three sets of Jesus sayings make clear that, far from loosening the law's stance on sex, Jesus intensified the ethical demand in this area: (a) Jesus' stance on divorce and remarriage (Mk 10:1–12; also Mt 5:32 and the parallel in Luke 16:18; and Paul's citation of Jesus' position in 1 Cor 7:10–11); (b) Jesus' remark about adultery of the heart (Mt 5:27–28); and (c) Jesus' statement about removing body parts as preferable to being thrown into hell (Mt 5:29–30 and Mk 9:43–48) which, based on the context in Matthew as well as rabbinic parallels, primarily has to do with sexual immorality. Simply put, sex mattered to Jesus. Jesus did not broaden the range of acceptable sexual expression; he narrowed it. And he thought that unrepentant, repetitive deviation from this norm could get a person thrown into hell."[8]

Jesus may well be referring to the subject in Matthew's Gospel when He asks the crowd about John the Baptist. "What did you go out into the wilderness to behold? . . . a man clothed in soft raiment? . . . those who wear soft raiment are in kings' houses." The translation from the Greek is deeply significant here. The Greek word *malakos* means "soft" or "tender," but could easily signify the word "effeminate." It's an issue open to question. What is not in question are His comments regarding God's plan for creation, and His use of Genesis, also in Matthew's Gospel: "Have you not read that he who made them from the beginning made them male and female . . . and the two shall become one?" This is extremely important. Beyond the negative, the condemning, and the prohibitive, is the planned, the desired, the required, and the blessed. Catholics believe that God has a plan, with at its heart the relationship between the creator and the creature. The very construction of the human person, the body itself, is designed to procreate and designed male and female to meet in the sexual act to procreate, which is of course essential to the furthering of the human race. This is a biological fact, but also a Catholic reality. Catholics believe that design is intelligent and always for a reason, not random and an accident. Christ affirms this in His address to the crowd.

This is conveniently forgotten, and often aggressively ignored, by modern gay writers, who go further and suggest that far from condemning homosexuality, Jesus the orthodox Jew, strict moralist, and the man who told His followers that sin led to damnation was in fact a homosexual Himself. This offensive flummery centres on Jesus and the person described in the Gospel of John as the "disciple whom he loved." The same nonsense is attempted concerning the relationship between King David and Jonathan, suggesting that they were not brotherly friends but gay lovers. It's absurd to the point of hilarity, and of course deeply insulting. Putting aside that fact that this revisionism began only in very recent times and coincides precisely with the gay rights campaign, it defies basic logic. Homosexuality was quite clearly considered a sin and even a crime in the ancient Jewish world. The Old Testament and the Jews regarded David as a hero and an icon, and modern Jewish people still do. Yet according to some authors that same Old Testament writes of King David having a homosexual affair with Jonathan. But if it was homosexuality, it would never have been mentioned at all; that it is referred to and even in some detail proves precisely that it was the very opposite of such a relationship, was platonic and entirely innocent. Gay activists have similarly tried to tarnish the Roman Catholic leader and author Cardinal Newman by claiming he was a homosexual, especially when he was beatified in 2010.[9] The claim is that he was the gay lover of his friend Hurrell Froude. But Newman wrote about his love for Froude and never tried to hide it; would someone who publicly condemned homosexuality, living in a society and at a time when homosexuality was illegal, have made his sexuality so public and known? Obviously not. It's a form of clumsy proselytizing, and all the worse and disrespectful when applied to Jesus, whom Catholics regard as the Son of God.

Back to that person, Jesus Christ. The Greek word *agapan*, which is used in the Gospel of John, means a pure love and one totally lacking in passion. There are many other Greek words that could have been used such as *eran* or *storghein* that would be far more plausible if homosexuality was in any way implied. Once again, we have to apply logic. If any of this were true, it's not remotely possible that other people would not have suggested it at the time, particularly critics of Jesus and Christianity. In the early church, Jewish and Roman opponents of Christianity were searching for any attack they could find, from suggesting that Jesus's mother was raped by a Roman soldier to claiming that the guards of His tomb had been bribed. If he had been homosexual, the church would have collapsed or would never have even begun. But the accusation was never made, by those who knew Him, those who loved Him, or those who hated Him. Never suggested because it would have been a patently absurd thing to do.

So if this approach won't work, just make something up. In 1973 Professor Morton Smith of the University of Harvard published a fragment, a mere twenty lines, of what he described as the "Secret Gospel of Mark." And, surprise surprise, he explained that it was clearly supportive of homosexuality. These types of spurious and crassly tendentious allegations have become a virtual industry, with famous person after famous person and text after text suddenly revealed as being gay, pro-gay, or gay-positive. The love that dare not speak its name transformed into the love that really should give it a rest. The Morton Smith examples concern Jesus raising a young man from death in a tomb in Bethany. "The young man, looking at him, loved him. . . . Six days later . . . in the evening the young man joined him wearing a cloth of linen over his naked body; that night he stayed with him, and Jesus taught him the mystery of the kingdom of God." Which seems to be extremely significant and even transforming, until and unless you think about it just a little. The manuscript in question is only two centuries old, which is more than 250 years after the first printing press. This is vital, because the discipline of textual analysis and proving literary authenticity is extremely sceptical and even dismissive of post–printing-press documents that suddenly appear and seem to rewrite history. Nobody has ever seen the original of this text, and, anyway, it seems to be little more than a combining and confusing of the stories from the Gospels of Mark and John concerning the famous story of the raising of the tomb of Lazarus. The last and best word about this is probably that of the Jewish and certainly non-Catholic and not even particularly sympathetic scholar Jacob Neusner, who described the Morton Smith argument as "the forgery of the century." Even so, it is used repeatedly to support the idea that Christ was a homosexual and so would have supported same-sex marriage. The future Church needs to become familiar with these arguments. They may be tedious, they may be irritating, but they are also effective.

Beyond actual Scripture, the Church Fathers, those who shaped and formed the Roman Catholic Church in its early days, shape the Church today, and will continue to shape the future Church, were unfailing in their opinions. The Didache, or the Teaching of the Twelve Apostles, is a late first-century or early second-century Christian treatise and is considered one of the most important Christian documents outside of the Bible. "You shall not commit murder, you shall not commit adultery, you shall not commit pederasty, you shall not commit fornication, you shall not steal, you shall not practice magic, you shall not practice witchcraft, you shall not murder a child by abortion nor kill one that has been born" (Didache 2:2). It's essential to note here that homosexuality is not alone and that abortion and adultery – both common today and both largely heterosexual in nature – are also condemned, but that nor is it excluded. Justin Martyr was an early Christian apologist and is now considered a Catholic saint. Once again, he does not single out "sodomy" but he insists on including it in his litany of sins. "[W]e have been taught that to expose newly-born children is the part of wicked men; and this we have been taught lest we should do anyone harm and lest we should sin against God, first, because we see that almost all so exposed (not only the girls, but also the males) are brought up to prostitution. And for this pollution a multitude of females and hermaphrodites, and those who commit unmentionable iniquities, are found in every nation. And you receive the hire of these, and duty and taxes from them, whom you ought to exterminate from your realm. And anyone who uses such persons, besides the godless and infamous and impure intercourse, may possibly be having intercourse with his own child, or relative, or brother. And there are some who prostitute even their own children and wives, and some are openly mutilated for the purpose of sodomy; and they refer these mysteries to the mother of the gods" (First Apology 27 [AD 151]).[10]

Clement of Alexandria was a Christian apologist and saint, who lived in the late second century. He wrote: "All honor to that king of the Scythians, whoever Anacharsis was, who shot with an arrow one of his subjects who imitated among the Scythians the mystery of the mother of the gods . . . condemning him as having become effeminate among the Greeks, and a teacher of the disease of effeminacy to the rest of the Scythians" (Exhortation to the Greeks 2 [AD 190]). He continues: "It is not, then, without reason that the poets call him [Hercules] a cruel wretch and a nefarious scoundrel. It were tedious to recount his adulteries of all sorts, and debauching of boys. For your gods did not even abstain from boys, one having loved Hylas, another Hyacinthus, another Pelops, another Chrysippus, another Ganymede. Let such gods as these be worshipped by your wives, and let them pray that their husbands be such as these – so temperate; that, emulating them in the same practices, they may be like the gods. Such gods let your boys be trained to worship, that they may grow up to be men with the accursed likeness of fornication on them received from the gods." And "The fate of the Sodomites was judgment to those who had done wrong, instruction to those who hear. The Sodomites having, through much luxury, fallen into uncleanness, practicing adultery shamelessly, and burning with insane love for boys; the All-seeing Word, whose notice those who commit impieties cannot escape, cast his eye on them. Nor did the sleepless guard of humanity observe their licentiousness in silence; but dissuading us from the imitation of them, and training us up to his own temperance, and falling on some sinners, lest lust being unavenged, should break loose from all the restraints of fear, ordered Sodom to be burned, pouring forth a little of the sagacious fire on licentiousness; lest lust, through want of punishment, should throw wide the gates to those that were rushing into voluptuousness. Accordingly, the just punishment of the Sodomites became to men an image of the salvation which is well calculated for men. For those who have not committed like sins with those who are punished, will never receive a like punishment."[11]

Tertullian was a Christian writer from Carthage in Africa who lived in the late first and early second century: He wrote: "[A]ll other frenzies of the lusts which exceed the laws of nature, and are impious toward both [human] bodies and the sexes, we banish, not only from the threshold but also from all shelter of the Church, for they are not sins so much as monstrosities" (Modesty 4 [AD 220]). The laws of nature, which will be discussed later, are fundamental to the Christian understanding of sexuality and marriage. The body is designed in a certain way, with certain functions, and homosexual union exceeds these functions and breaks these laws. The Roman theologian and priest Novatian: "[God forbade the Jews to eat certain foods for symbolic reasons:] For that in fishes the roughness of scales is regarded as constituting their cleanness; rough, and rugged, and unpolished, and substantial, and grave manners are approved in men; while those that are without scales are unclean, because trifling, and fickle, and faithless, and effeminate manners are disapproved. Moreover, what does the law mean when it . . . forbids the swine to be taken for food? It assuredly reproves a life filthy and dirty, and delighting in the garbage of vice. . . . Or when it forbids the hare? It rebukes men deformed into women" (The Jewish Foods 3 [AD 250]).

Cyprian was bishop of Carthage, born in North Africa in the early third century. He was eventually martyred. "[T]urn your looks to the abominations, not less to be deplored, of another kind of spectacle. . . . Men are emasculated, and all the pride and vigor of their sex is effeminated in the disgrace of their enervated body; and he is more pleasing there who has most completely broken down the man into the woman. He grows into praise by virtue of his crime; and the more he is degraded, the more skillful he is considered to be. Such a one is looked upon – oh shame! – and looked upon with pleasure. . . . Nor is there wanting authority for the enticing abomination . . . that Jupiter of theirs [is] not more supreme in dominion than in vice,

inflamed with earthly love in the midst of his own thunders . . .
now breaking forth by the help of birds to violate the purity of
boys. And now put the question: Can he who looks upon such
things be healthy-minded or modest? Men imitate the gods
whom they adore, and to such miserable beings their crimes
become their religion" (Letters 1:8 [AD 253]).

Arnobius of Sicca wrote slightly later, but still in the early
days of the emerging Christian church: "[T]he mother of the
gods loved [the boy Attis] exceedingly, because he was of most
surpassing beauty; and Acdestis [the son of Jupiter] who was his
companion, as he grew up fondling him, and bound to him by
wicked compliance with his lust. . . . Afterwards, under the
influence of wine, he [Attis] admits that he is . . . loved by
Acdestis. . . . Then Midas, king of Pessinus, wishing to withdraw
the youth from so disgraceful an intimacy, resolves to give him
his own daughter in marriage. . . . Acdestis, bursting with rage
because of the boy's being torn from himself and brought to seek
a wife, fills all the guests with frenzied madness; the Phrygians
shriek, panic-stricken at the appearance of the gods. . . . [Attis]
too, now filled with furious passion, raving frantically and
tossed about, throws himself down at last, and under a pine tree
mutilates himself, saying, 'Take these, Acdestis, for which you
have stirred up so great and terribly perilous commotions'"
(Against the Pagans 5:6–7 [AD 305]).

Eusebius of Caesarea was one of the most important early
Christian writers. He was Bishop of Caesarea in Palestine and is
considered the father of Church history: "[H]aving forbidden
all unlawful marriage, and all unseemly practice, and the union
of women with women and men with men, he [God] adds: 'Do
not defile yourselves with any of these things; for in all these
things the nations were defiled, which I will drive out before

you. And the land was polluted, and I have recompensed [their] iniquity upon it, and the land is grieved with them that dwell upon it' [Lv 18:24–25]" (Proof of the Gospel 4:10 [AD 319]).

Basil the Great was a Greek bishop, a doctor of the church, and the father of communal monasticism. Fourth-century Christians looked to him for instruction and guidance: "He who is guilty of unseemliness with males will be under discipline for the same time as adulterers" (Letters 217:62 [AD 367]). And "If you [O, monk] are young in either body or mind, shun the companionship of other young men and avoid them as you would a flame. For through them the enemy has kindled the desires of many and then handed them over to eternal fire, hurling them into the vile pit of the five cities under the pretense of spiritual love. . . . At meals take a seat far from other young men. In lying down to sleep let not their clothes be near yours, but rather have an old man between you. When a young man converses with you, or sings psalms facing you, answer him with eyes cast down, lest perhaps by gazing at his face you receive a seed of desire sown by the enemy and reap sheaves of corruption and ruin. Whether in the house or in a place where there is no one to see your actions, be not found in his company under the pretense either of studying the divine oracles or of any other business whatsoever, however necessary" (The Renunciation of the World [AD 373]).

John Chrysostom was a late fourth-century theologian, the Archbishop of Constantinople, and an extremely important church father. He is a saint and doctor of the church: "[The pagans] were addicted to the love of boys, and one of their wise men made a law that pederasty . . . should not be allowed to slaves, as if it was an honorable thing; and they had houses for this purpose, in which it was openly practiced. And if all that was done among them was related, it would be seen that they openly outraged nature, and there was none to restrain them. . . . As for their passion for boys, whom they called their paedica, it is not fit to be named" (Homilies on Titus 5 [AD 390]). And "[Certain men in church] come in gazing about at the beauty of women; others curious about the blooming youth of boys. After this, do you not marvel that [lightning] bolts are not launched [from heaven], and all these things are not plucked up from their foundations? For worthy both of thunderbolts and hell are the things that are done; but God, who is long-suffering, and of great mercy, forbears awhile his wrath, calling you to repentance and amendment" (Homilies on Matthew 3:3 [AD 391]).

He also wrote in the same book, "All of these affections [in Rom 1:26–27] . . . were vile, but chiefly the mad lust after males; for the soul is more the sufferer in sins, and more dishonored than the body in diseases" (Homilies on Romans 4 [AD391]). In the same work, "And sundry other books of the philosophers one may see full of this disease. But we do not therefore say that the thing was made lawful, but that they who received this law were pitiable, and objects for many tears. For these are treated in the same way as women that play the whore. Or rather their plight is more miserable. For in the case of the one the intercourse, even if lawless, is yet according to nature; but this is contrary both to law and nature. For even if there were no hell, and no punishment had been threatened, this would be worse than any punishment."

Finally, St. Augustine of Hippo, one of and perhaps the most important theorist and theologian in Christian history: "[T]hose shameful acts against nature, such as were committed in Sodom, ought everywhere and always to be detested and punished. If all nations were to do such things, they would be held guilty of the same crime by the law of God, which has not made men so that they should use one another in this way" (Confessions 3:8:15 [AD 400]).[12]

This is a mere selection, from just the first few centuries of Catholicism. The same view is repeated again and again in the following centuries, right through to and including modern times. In modern times, the debate and the discussion is more heated and angry than it was two thousand years ago, for a whole series of reasons, but heat and anger are not sufficient reason to tamper with an ancient truth. Part of the modern challenge is finding a way to have the culture actually listen to the Catholic position in the first place, or to listen without distorting what is actually said. In the summer of 2012, the Roman Catholic Bishop of Aberdeen, Hugh Gilbert, responded to a proposal by the Scottish government in Edinburgh to extend and expand civil union into full marriage, in spite of the fact that polls showed that the vast majority of Scottish people were satisfied with civil unions and were opposed to any further reforms. Bishop Gilbert was immediately and horribly pilloried as an extremist. But all he said in essence was that the argument for legalising same-sex marriage was based at heart on a dangerous precedent: if we believe that marriage requires only that people love each other and want to be committed to each other, what is to stop a man who loves two or three women and wants to be committed to them as well forming a polygamous marriage? Or, he continued, a niece may also love her uncle and be committed to him, or a nephew to an aunt. Should, then, the love and commitment underpinning same-sex marriage lead the government to consider legalizing polygamy and incest? He was merely exposing the flawed thesis behind same-sex marriage, and one does not have to agree with the argument to appreciate the logic. But as the noted blogger and priest Father

Tim Finigan said at the time, "Nowhere in his argument does he say that same-sex marriage is of the same moral character as bigamy or incest. Nor does he say that same-sex marriage will lead to bigamy or incest. He is pointing out that the argument used to justify same-sex marriage could equally well be used to justify bigamy or incest and that it is therefore fatally flawed." Yet almost immediately the Bishop made his comment, the director of the Equality Network, an organization promoting gay marriage in Britain, told the media, "We are very disappointed the Bishop of Aberdeen should choose to compare same-sex marriage to polygamy and incest. That is offensive and uncalled for." But this is not what the Bishop said at all. He didn't compare same-sex marriage to polygamy and incest but demonstrated that the argument used to justify same-sex marriage could also be used to justify polygamy and incest. The gay online newspaper Pink News then joined the chorus of dishonesty with "Catholic Bishop: Government should make incest legal if it really believes in equality." No, no, no. That's not what he said, not what he intended to say, and not what any rational, intelligent person would construe from what he had said. So, damned if you do, damned if you don't; which is, I suppose, entirely appropriate and fitting language for such a discussion.

The Roman Catholic Church's Catechism – published in French in 1992 and in English in 1994 – spends a great deal of time dealing with issues of homosexuality and is worth quoting at some length. It will not satisfy, let alone please, everyone, and terms such as *disordered* and *depravity* are jarring to many. I urge people, however, to appreciate how the text differentiates between an act and a person, and how it calls for understanding and respect. Catholics believe that we are far more than our sexuality, and that this aspect of our being constitutes just one factor in the human person. The catechism, by the way, will stand as a foundational document for the future Church, for the long-term future. We might as well, so to speak, get used to it.

"Homosexuality refers to relations between men or between women who experience an exclusive or predominant sexual attraction toward persons of the same sex. It has taken a great variety of forms through the centuries and in different cultures. Its psychological genesis remains largely unexplained. Basing itself on Sacred Scripture, which presents homosexual acts as acts of grave depravity, tradition has always declared that 'homosexual acts are intrinsically disordered.' They are contrary to the natural law. They close the sexual act to the gift of life. They do not proceed from a genuine affective and sexual complementarity. Under no circumstances can they be approved. The number of men and women who have deep-seated homosexual tendencies is not negligible. This inclination, which is objectively disordered, constitutes for most of them a trial. They must be accepted with respect, compassion, and sensitivity. Every sign of unjust discrimination in their regard should be avoided. These persons are called to fulfill God's will in their lives and, if they are Christians, to unite to the sacrifice of the Lord's Cross the difficulties they may encounter from their condition. Homosexual persons are called to chastity. By the virtues of self-mastery that teach them inner freedom, at times by the support of disinterested friendship, by prayer and sacramental grace, they can and should gradually and resolutely approach Christian perfection. Fecundity is a gift, an end of marriage, for conjugal love naturally tends to be fruitful. A child does not come from outside as something added on to the mutual love of the spouses, but springs from the very heart of that mutual giving, as its fruit and fulfillment. So the Church, which is 'on the side of life, teaches that 'it is necessary that each and every marriage act remain ordered per se to the procreation of human life.' This particular doctrine, expounded on numerous occasions by the Magisterium, is based on the inseparable connection, established by God, which man on his own initiative may not break, between the unitive significance and the procreative significance which are both inherent to the marriage act.

"Called to give life, spouses share in the creative power and fatherhood of God. Married couples should regard it as their proper mission to transmit human life and to educate their children; they should realize that they are thereby cooperating with the love of God the Creator and are, in a certain sense, its interpreters. They will fulfill this duty with a sense of human and Christian responsibility. A particular aspect of this responsibility concerns the regulation of procreation. For just reasons, spouses may wish to space the births of their children. It is their duty to make certain that their desire is not motivated by selfishness but is in conformity with the generosity appropriate to responsible parenthood. Moreover, they should conform their behavior to the objective criteria of morality: When it is a question of harmonizing married love with the responsible transmission of life, the morality of the behavior does not depend on sincere intention and evaluation of motives alone; but it must be determined by objective criteria, criteria drawn from the nature of the person and his acts, criteria that respect the total meaning of mutual self-giving and human procreation in the context of true love; this is possible only if the virtue of married chastity is practiced with sincerity of heart. By safeguarding both these essential aspects, the unitive and the procreative, the conjugal act preserves in its fullness the sense of true mutual love and its orientation toward man's exalted vocation to parenthood."

So, where do we go now, and what happens next? More of the same unfortunately, but with an increased sense of entitlement and triumphalism. The future Church cannot change its teachings regarding these issues because they go to the quintessence of creation, God, salvation, natural law, and the foundation of the Catholic understanding of creation and what it means to be a child of God. It is so much more than sexuality. Mainline Protestant churches are beginning to accept same-sex marriage either completely or in piecemeal stages, and those trying to hold the line on traditional Christian teaching are often coming to realize that the only home for them is the Catholic Church. Many converts to Catholicism from other churches explain this as their primary reasons for crossing the Tiber; not that it was centrally important to *them*, but that it was all-important to those who insisted on pursuing it. It is not the issue itself but what lies beneath it that is leading to this exodus of traditional Christians. They will tell you that the gay-marriage issue is merely a symptom of a far greater malaise, where ostensible Christians cannot recite the basic creeds of the faith. The Church of the future will see ever more converts fleeing as they realize that their churches will not hold true to ancient teaching. Even many evangelical churches, and certainly some younger evangelical leaders, are watering down their statements and teachings, such is the pressure to conform. They have concluded that to be listened to as Christians, they have to transform the Christian message on this vitally important subject. So in a very non-Catholic response they are rewriting the faith not due to pressure of Scripture but to pressure of society. The Catholic Church has never changed its views for the sake of popularity or the more credible and even laudable reasons of reaching people; the lesson is that this is generally the wisest policy, and always the only genuinely Christian one. The Church of the future will be as counter-cultural as it was in its earliest days and will be probably far more loathed and victimized because of this than it was, say, in the 1950s and 60s. Pope Benedict predicted a smaller but more Catholic Church; perhaps when it comes to this subject in particular we can predict a more Catholic and more persecuted one as well.

II

ABORTION AND BIRTH CONTROL

IF THE FUTURE CHURCH is going to face particular pressure to change concerning the same-sex marriage issue, it will face almost equally intense hostility due to teaching on abortion, and in particular on birth control and so-called family planning. The former will bring the Church into conflict largely with the secular world, the latter with many Catholics as well. I suppose we have to first ponder whether this is one question or two, but once we explore the theme and its foundations what becomes obvious is that the distinction between abortion and artificial birth control is a false one in a Catholic context, while remaining an influential one in secular culture. There are few – though an increasing number of – serious Catholics who see a future Church that condones abortion, but a far larger number of Catholics – even within the clergy and episcopate – who look to a future where birth control is allowed within Catholic teaching. I speak here not of casual Catholics who pick and choose what they want to believe, but of otherwise serious believers, and even important and influential voices, who think that the Church has to adapt its teaching concerning contraception for any number of reasons. For that reason, we'll deal with abortion first and contraception later.

The Catholic Church is simply not going to reform it position on the subject of abortion, even though the surrounding culture and even other Christian bodies have accepted as a self-evident right the ability of a woman to have a doctor kill her unborn child. In 2007 in a speech in Argentina, Pope Francis, then Archbishop of Buenos Aires, said: "We aren't in agreement with the death penalty. But in Argentina, the penalty does exist. A child conceived by the rape of a mentally ill or retarded woman can be condemned to death." That's pretty strong and uncompromising language. As it was when he said, "Protect the unborn against abortion even if they persecute you, calumniate you, set traps for you, take you to court or kill you." Pope Francis has also been resolute in his criticism of politicians who claim to be Catholic but support abortion, a topic that will be discussed at some length in the chapter on the future Church refusing Communion and the separation of church and state. Nicolas Lafferriere, head of Argentina's Center for Bioethics, Person and Family, said, "Those of us who work for life and family in Argentina have always felt ourselves to be supported and promoted by Cardinal Bergoglio. On the one hand, he has promoted the dignity of each woman and especially of women during pregnancy." So Pope Francis is in no way going to change Catholic teaching regarding the unborn, and the future Church will not compromise on its commitment to life. How could it, in that this is about as fundamental a moral teaching as it gets and begins in Scripture itself. Psalm 139 has this: "For you created my inmost being; you knit me together in my mother's womb. I praise you because I am fearfully and wonderfully made; your works are wonderful, I know that full well. My frame was not hidden from you when I was made in the secret place. When I was woven together in the depths of the earth, your eyes saw my unformed body. All the days ordained for me were written in your book before one of them came to be." Job has this: "Did not he who made me in the womb make them? Did not the same one form us both within our mothers?" and Jeremiah, "Before I formed you in the womb I knew you, before you were born I set you apart; I appointed you as a prophet to the nations."

Catholicism, however, is not a faith that forms its teachings exclusively around Scripture, which is an issue that we will, again, discuss in greater detail in the chapter concerning Papal supremacy and the future of authority in the Catholic Church. The continuing theme of Catholic teaching, which has always informed the Church and will continue to do so in the future Church, is natural law. Science is very much a product of natural law, a sibling in fact, and science tells us that a child is a child from its earliest stage. At the moment of conception, a male sperm unites with a female ovum to fertilize it, and the single-celled organism formed is called a zygote, an intricate and sophisticated repository of biological information of both parents. Fertilization occurs in the Fallopian tube, and shortly afterwards cells move to the uterine wall of the womb. Within the next twenty-four to forty-eight hours, the tiny zygote multiplies at an extraordinary rate and becomes what is called a blastocyst or a placenta, containing 150 cells. This is the embryo and will last until the eighth week of development. From the eighth week until birth, the word *fetus* is used. One month after conception, the eyes, ears, and respiratory stem are developing, and three weeks later the baby is sucking its thumb. A week later the heart can be felt beating and the following week the baby can grip and bend its fingers. Eleven weeks after conception, there is steady breathing and then the baby will be able to swallow the amniotic fluid. Around two weeks after this, around fourteen weeks from conception, the baby can taste, and between sixteen and twenty weeks the baby can hear, including hearing its mother's heartbeats. At twenty-three weeks after conception, the baby is sleeping regularly, and six months after conception the baby's sweat glands are functioning. The following month the baby kicks, stretches, performs somersaults. From this point on, there is considerable weight gain, and at around nine months the baby is born and, suddenly, has a right to life, liberty, education, free speech, health care, assembly, and whatever else.[1] It all seems rather arbitrary that these secondary rights are suddenly given to a person who up until that point had no right under law to be born and to not be killed.

At conception a child has a unique DNA and genomic character and is already unlike anyone who has been conceived or born before or anyone who will be conceived or born afterwards. It is a distinct human life and like all human life in a civilized society should have a right to exist.[2] But for more than a generation now, the Catholic position has been largely ignored in the great debate over life and its meaning, and frankly there is no reason to believe that this will change in the future. The future Church is not going to change its position merely because the usual arguments are repeated, as they have been for several decades now. Of course a woman has the choice to do whatever she wants with her own body to almost unlimited extent, but she does not have the right to do harm to a distinct person within her. And yes, Catholics know that an unborn child cannot survive outside of the womb, but then a fully developed newborn child, or for that matter an injured or sick adult, will die quickly if left without help from another person. Viability outside of the womb is a convenient but unreliable argument in defence of abortion. After three months of growth, there is really no new serious or profound development in an unborn baby, and while at nine months the unborn child is obviously more mature than it was earlier, this is in fact little different from a ten-year-old being more mature than a two-year-old, yet we wouldn't attribute more humanity and human rights to a ten-year-old child merely because it was a few years older than its sibling. We certainly wouldn't argue that it had a greater right to live.

One of the challenges Catholics have faced in the past, and it's certain that this will be the case in the future, is that while they feel instinctively that abortion is wrong, they haven't been able to articulate a reasoned, seasoned response to people who often obsess about the issue, to a far greater extent than Catholics ever do, in spite of what they are accused of. They are often asked, as a starting point, why it is that if abortion is so wrong it is primarily Catholics who oppose it. Why not everyone, runs the attack question; why would it not be obvious to all that this was a crime and a tragedy? Let's consider the example of the tragic death of a spouse. It is objectively a terrible thing, a horror, but only the surviving partner would feel it with particular sting and with particular agony. Equally, abortion is objectively a terrible thing, a horror, but only those who are part of an institution given to us by God, the Catholic Church, feel the pain especially strongly, because they are part of that circle of humanity that includes all and empathizes with the loss of all. This is not arrogance but understanding. Proclaiming truth even at the risk of being accused of arrogance and judgmentalism, by the way, is something that the future Church will have to not only get used to but also learn to ignore. Spending too much time listening to empty accusations, let alone responding to them, is enervating and usually pointless.

But how should Catholics, how should the future Church, respond to those who demand that Catholicism should change its teaching on abortion because of pregnancies that result from cases of rape and incest? The question will always be a digression, in that these tragic circumstances are the cause – thank goodness – of extremely few abortions. Let's be sensible and direct here: the question is asked not to enlighten the debate but to make Catholics appear extreme and lacking in empathy and sympathy. Catholics should ask in return if those who support abortion in these rare cases would oppose it when rape and incest are not the causes of pregnancy. It would be a redundant question, of course, because those asking it are invariably solidly in favour of what are now euphemistically and misleadingly termed abortion rights. The arguments used in the past will continue in the future, because there is nothing new that the supporters of abortion can throw at the Church. Another is that without legal and accessible abortion, there will be a plague of backstreet abortions and women will be horribly injured and even die. There were indeed backstreet abortions, but the solution to this is not to make abortion legal but to stop backstreet abortions. Remember, babies always die when these procedures take place, in whatever part of the street they occur. We are also only now beginning to understand just how much psychological, emotional, and physical trauma is brought about when women allow their unborn babies to be killed. This is an aspect of the abortion debate that has not been sufficiently discussed in the past but has to be stressed in the future by Catholics as more information comes to light.

The future Church will also have more access to the increasing amount of evidence linking abortion to cancer. Feminist and medical doctor Angela Lanfranchi is one of many voices now speaking out on the links between not only abortion and breast cancer, but the medical and carcinogenic dangers of contraceptive use. She will most certainly be joined by many other medics and experts in the years to come. "In the course of my professional career, I noticed that there were a whole lot more young women with breast cancer than there should be and that the incidence had gone from 1 in 12 when I graduated medical school to 1 in 8 in just 30 years. When I looked into risk factors for this, it became clear that oral contraceptives, induced abortion, and delayed first pregnancies accounted for a good number of these early breast cancers. Having patients in their 20s with breast cancer and seeing them die in their 30s made me want to try to do something that would prevent those cancers," she wrote.

"To that end, in 1999 I co-founded the Breast Cancer Prevention Institute which educates the public and medical professionals on the risks and prevention of breast cancer. The old feminism sought equality with men through complete reproductive control using oral contraceptives and the necessary back up of abortion. Without them, women felt they could never climb the corporate ladder. It was as if women needed to live their lives with the same sexual license as men in order to achieve equality. We thought we could have children whenever we wanted no matter our age. We could even have them without a husband. We just needed to buy a deposit from a sperm bank. If we only knew then what we know now: that oral contraceptives are a Group 1 carcinogen for breast, cervical and liver cancer; that abortion causes breast cancer, premature births and serious psychological problems; that women need husbands as children need fathers; that sexual intercourse sets off hormonal changes within us that bonds us to our mate. The theories of the old feminism, no matter how strongly or earnestly embraced, could not change the hard wiring in our brains or in our hearts. It is hard to look back and admit we were so wrong about so many things."[3]

Then we have the perennial criticism that abortion is a women's issue and only to be discussed and defined by women.

It's a logical fallacy on numerous levels but rather implodes at its most fundamental level when we remember that many of the most active opponents of abortion are women. But more to the point, abortion is either right or wrong, and the gender of the person making the argument about the issue is entirely irrelevant. To assume that women can and must believe only one set of views about abortion is not a feminist argument but its very contrary. This is not about demanding but allowing, not about curtailing rights but expanding life. No woman should be obliged to raise a child, but no person has a right to kill a child.

Gender bias does, however, come into play in the abortion debate because abortion leads to far more baby girls being aborted than baby boys. Modern technology has met with archaic gender preferences, and in parts of the Third World in particular, and in diaspora communities in Europe and North America, women are aborting babies if they are female and keeping them if they're male. Rather a bitter paradox for feminist ideology. In spite of what we term progress, this is an increasing rather than diminishing phenomenon, and the future Church will be one of the few institutions taking a resolute stand against it. It's all deeply paradoxical and confusing for supporters of abortion, because if the unborn child is genuinely nothing more than tissue with no rights – which has to be the case for any civilized defence of abortion – this should not be an issue. But it most certainly is an issue, even among those who would otherwise describe themselves as being pro-choice, meaning that they've been living something of an ideological lie. They may argue that the specific killing of unborn little girls is morally irrelevant but viscerally they react extremely strongly and even emotionally to it because they know, perhaps for the first time, that it is wrong. They know that the victims are girls, and girls being killed purely because of their sex. Self-identification can change hearts, minds, and lives, and the future Church has to stress that the pro-life position is an extension of the Catholic defence of the most vulnerable in society: women, the handicapped, people of colour – all the prime victims of abortion.

We claim to be an enlightened age, more progressive and tolerant than at any time in the past and certainly more diverse and kind than the Catholic-based societies of old that we so like to use as examples of how we have evolved. We will provide facilities for handicapped people and congratulate ourselves on how we care for them. Yet abortion now deliberately targets those whose handicap can be detected in the womb, as many disabilities can be now and as many more will be in the future. Children with Down syndrome, for example, are being aborted at a grotesque rate, and there may come a time when we hardly ever see such people in society, where few if any children will even know what a Down syndrome person looked like. On the one hand, we tell people with physical and mental challenges that they are equal and that everybody has equal worth but simultaneously we offer, allow, and sometimes encourage – it is standard for a doctor to inform a mother if an unborn baby has what is known as a "defect" and offer the grand euphemism of an "alternative to birth" – the removal of babies who may grow up looking a little different from the rest of the population. The fight against this new form of eugenics and social engineering is an essential aspect of Catholic outreach in the coming years.

One of the few organized groups trying to change the Church's teaching concerning abortion is the grotesquely and misleadingly named Catholics for a Free Choice. The group was founded in 1972 and, although representing very few people, enjoys a prominence in media circles that far outweighs its genuine significance. Sadly, there is no sign that the organization is going away, and if anything it is gaining a foothold in the debate, often being included in mainstream media as a "balance" to the Catholic pro-life viewpoint, as if this were a genuine point of disagreement. Catholics for a Free Choice boast eight thousand members, although there is no evidence that they have even this many. They do, however, have an annual budget of almost a million dollars, which according to records filed with the Inland Revenue Service is partly provided by the Playboy Foundation. In other words, a group claiming to be faithfully Catholic receives some of its money from people dedicated to publishing degrading pornography and helping to reduce sexuality to its most loveless form, and to provide artificial fantasies to, among others, married men so that they can emotionally betray their wives.

Beyond this fringe group of ostensible Catholics and their obsessions, let us look at the subject of embryonic stem-cell research, an area where critics of the Church and those who are anxious that Catholicism should change it teachings have been at best disingenuous and perhaps even downright dishonest. Only weeks after Pope Francis assumed office, a conference was held in Rome on the subject of stem-cell research and regenerative medicine. The conference was supported by the Vatican and enthusiastically approved of stem-cell research, leading to headlines that the new Papacy would have a dramatically different attitude toward the issue than the Church of the past, and that Catholicism was entering a new, enlightened age. It was part sloppy journalism, part wishful thinking, part woeful ignorance of Catholic theology. The conference, backed by Pope Francis and his cardinals, was called to discuss not embryonic but adult stem cells and the essential research that was taking place in this area, often through the efforts of Catholic doctors. As the conference stated:

"The human embryo is a living member of the human species who, like every one of us, is always in development. Every human being possesses an equal moral dignity and has a fundamental Right to Life. This is true no matter what age or stage of our development, degree of dependence upon others (we are all dependent upon others) or the opinion of others as to our 'worth'. We are not products we are persons. The Vatican expressed it this way in 2008, 'the use of human embryos or fetuses as an object of experimentation constitutes a crime against their dignity as human beings who have a right to the same respect owed to a child once born, just as to every person.' (Congregation for the Doctrine of the Faith, Instruction Dignitas Personae on Certain Bioethical Questions). Among the worst examples of using language to deceive and hide the truth is the failure to differentiate between human embryonic stem cell research and adult stem cell research. I have personally concluded that blurring these two very different areas of medical research may be an intentional act on the part of some who are hell bent on killing human embryonic persons for experimentation. Oh, I know, some people will gasp when they read such a strong statement. However, given the amazing breakthroughs occurring with adult stem cell research and the lack of coverage such advances are receiving, I am left with no alternative."

None of this should come as any type of surprise to anyone who understands the genuine rather than the tabloid history of the Church's involvement with science and scientific progress, a tradition that will doubtless continue. The science, rather than the emotion, is that stem cells can be taken from umbilical cords, the placenta, amniotic fluid, adult tissues and organs such as bone marrow, fat from liposuction, and regions of the nose. Stem cells can even be taken from cadavers up to twenty hours after death. There are in fact four different types of stem cell: embryonic stem cells, embryonic germ cells, umbilical cord stem cells, and adult stem cells. In that germ cells can be obtained from miscarriages that do not involve an abortion, the Church opposes only one of the three forms of stem-cell research, which may be surprising to some because the media has created the impression that if it were not for the Catholic Church's opposition to stem-cell research, any number of terrible diseases and illnesses would be solved almost overnight. Although enormous progress has been made with stem-cell research, there is not a case of a single person being cured through the use of embryonic cells, partly because adult stem cells are obviously part of an adult body whereas embryonic stem cells are obviously not.[4]

Another crucial part of the future of the Catholic Church will concern how it responds to allegations and theories that the world is overpopulated and that there will be no sustainable and viable future unless we control reproduction. It's an increasingly fashionable line of argument as it's part of the greater acceptance of climate change theories, some of them quite radical, and the acceptance of environmentalism. This is not the place for a deconstruction of the green movement – although some of the silencing of reasoned opposition to the "greening" of education, politics, and culture is of deep concern – but an opportunity to emphasize that the future Church will have an ever stronger relationship with, and influence, in the Third World, the developing world, the very countries accused by the secular West of being overpopulated and thus direct targets for abortion and contraception. Africa and Asia, runs the claim, have too many people, and as a consequence wealthy people have the right if not the duty to eliminate poor people. It may sound offensive, but it's nevertheless the essence of the population control movement.

One of the first reports from the Reuters news agency when the new Pope was announced made particular reference to this future Church reality: "African and Asian Catholics quickly identified with the new Pope's chosen name, in honor of St. Francis of Assisi, the 12th century saint who spurned wealth to pursue a life of poverty, as a sign of a fresh direction in the global Church. 'This will be the pope of the poor since he also comes from the far corners of the earth,' said Celso Dias, a 39-year-old law firm worker, as he stopped to pray at the whitewashed Santo Antonio da Polana Cathedral in the Mozambican capital Maputo. On the outskirts of Nigeria's commercial metropolis Lagos, Father Raymond Anoliefo, who runs a parish Church at Ibeju, said he was heartened to hear that Bergoglio had criticized the Argentine government for not doing enough to tackle poverty. 'The problems he has in his country are the same as ours: poverty, corruption,' he said. 'It's encouraging to have someone from the developing world. This is "our pope"'. In the Philippines, where more than 80 percent of the population are Catholic, Church leaders saw the selection of the first non-European pontiff in well over a millennium as a just recognition that the face of global Catholicism was changing. 'Pope Francis will have a grasp of what the Church faces in the Third World, where people are poor and yet the faith is growing fast,' said Jose Palma, the Archbishop of Cebu, the largest archdiocese in the Philippines. 'In contrast, we see a decline of our faith in the more affluent Europe,' he added." This is where the Church will flourish and where Catholic initiative will become increasingly obvious.

So the Third World will demand particular protection and devotion from the future Church, and that Church will have to embrace that challenge and that privilege. It will also be obliged to explain the poor to the rich, and the powerless to the powerful. It will have to tell the story of the people at the edges of society to the people at the centre, and to insist to the wealthy West that the world is not overpopulated at all but that, truth be told, the West is certainly greedy.

With the changing demographics of the world population, the future Church will be at the forefront of defending the emerging Africa and Asia, and reminding politicians that we in the West artificially divided up African regions, called them separate countries, and now wonder why they don't always function properly according to Western expectations. The Church has long questioned the international arms trade, for example, and in June 2013 the Permanent Observer of the Holy See to the United Nations, Archbishop Francis Chullikatt, issued a statement calling for the adoption of a treaty banning the transfer of arms when violations of humanitarian or human rights are taking place. "Archbishop Chullikatt emphasized the Holy See's belief that the good of the human person and the protection of human life and families should be the paramount concern in regulating the arms trade, rather than purely economic interests," reported Vatican Radio. "The Holy See, he said, 'has urged delegations to reorient the regulation of the trade in arms from one which is controlled through the lens of sheer economic interests to one which places overriding importance on human concerns and protecting human life and families'."

A poignant, shameful example of the different assumptions, expectations, and existences of people in the wealthy and the poor world: there is in Africa a wild-growing grass, *Hoodia gordonni*, that if sucked and chewed lessens the pains of hunger; it is given by mothers to their starving children. The grass has now been turned into capsules to be taken by obese people in the West as an appetite suppressant. The juxtaposition of one people forced by necessity to deal with terrible hunger and another by indulgence to control their inflated appetites is not only poignant but should be an embarrassment to the developed world. It's unjust, un-Catholic, and wrong. Yes, un-Catholic. Absolute equality is impossible and not even desirable but the obscene gap between wealthy and poor in the world is outrageous and has Western politicians concluding that the solution to Third World hunger issues is to reduce the population. No, the solution is to help them and allow them to feed themselves properly. It is always agonizing to see some of the champions of the permissive society in Hollywood – dramatically and hysterically anti-Catholic – making well-publicized trips to Africa and Asia to adopt a local baby. They may mean well – though the fashion for such adoption is sickening – but what they fail to appreciate is that the solution to child poverty is not to remove the children but to remove the poverty. This is what the Catholic Church has been demanding for decades, for a radical redistribution of wealth so that all of God's creatures can enjoy the comforts of a full belly and a long life.

In June 2013, in a strong prediction of what the future Church will proclaim in the area of food, fairness, and faith, Pope Francis spoke of "the culture of waste and the disposal" of goods and food, but also of people. He stressed that God has given humanity His creation and that it has to be cared for, but that the very epicentre of this is the human person: "Whereas today a child who dies of hunger is normal, if the stock market falls it is a tragedy." He continued, "Throwing food away is like stealing from the tables of the poor, the hungry. Human ecology and environmental ecology walk together."

Outlining that the Church does and will care about the environment, he explained why this was a Catholic issue: "When we talk about the environment, about creation, my thoughts turn to the first pages of the Bible, the Book of Genesis, which states that God placed man and woman on earth to cultivate and care for it (cf. 2:15). And the question comes to my mind: What does cultivating and caring for the earth mean? Are we truly cultivating and caring for creation? Or are we exploiting and neglecting it? The verb 'to cultivate' reminds me of the care that the farmer has for his land so that it bear fruit, and it is shared: how much attention, passion and dedication! Cultivating and caring for creation is God's indication given to each one of us not only at the beginning of history; it is part of His project; it means nurturing the world with responsibility and transforming it into a garden, a habitable place for everyone."

Everyone. Which is why the Catholic Church argues that it is not the size of the population that matters but how we treat that population. The Catholic commitment is to a world where skin colour and geographical location are less important than the Christian belief in the equal value of every human being. People do live in crowded conditions but they always have done so, no matter how small the population. It's human nature and economic reality that we assemble close together in order to exchange goods and maintain communal life and collective safety. There is nothing new in that at all. People actually occupy around 3 per cent of the earth's land surface. If 1,200 square feet was given to every person in the world, they would still all fit into an area the size of Texas – whether the Texans would object is an altogether different issue! World population growth is also declining. United Nations figures reveal that the 79 countries that make up 40 per cent of the world's population now have fertility rates too low to prevent population decline. The rate in Asia fell from 2.4 per cent between 1960 and 1965 to 1.5 per cent between 1990 and 1995. In Latin America and the Caribbean for the same dates, the rates fell from 2.75 to 1.70 per cent. Europe, of course, is rapidly losing its population altogether – 0.16 per cent between 1990 and 1995, which really means zero.[5]

Do note that when the Pope speaks of the environment and ecology, he emphasizes the centrality of the human person. The planet is to be respected not in itself, out of some pantheistic or pagan obsession, but because it is given to us by God, as a place where His loved creatures, man and woman, can live and be happy. It's a future Church environmentalism with a tradition stretching back to the earliest Church, and actually directly linked to Catholic understanding of sexuality, birth, and the natural rhythms of the body. Nothing new here, but something deliciously old. We can't be genuine environmentalists unless we appreciate the vitality and importance of the natural person, allowed to flourish in the way God intended. God created nature, we could argue, "the way nature intended." One of the most exciting culture clashes the future Church will take part in is outlining a new, human-based and holistic approach to ecology, moving far beyond the meagreness of a plant and animal devotion.

There was no better reminder of this than in early 2013 at the Women Deliver Conference in Kuala Lumpur, when the internationally acclaimed ethicist, author, and academic Peter Singer compared women and children to cows overgrazing a field and said that women's reproductive rights may one day have to be sacrificed for the environment. Singer is one of the most respected voices in this area of study and activism, and the conference was described as one of the most important of its kind in more than a decade. He said that while family planning was essential, "we ought to consider what other things there are that we can do . . . in order to try to stave off some of the worst consequences of the environmental catastrophe. It's possible of course, that we give women reproductive choices, that we meet the unmet need for contraception but that we find that the number of children that women *choose* to have is *still* such that population continues to rise in a way that causes environmental problems." He blamed procreation on women's ideology and – important this – their religion. He then compared a woman's right to have children to farmers having cows. "Turns out that the right to graze as many cows as you like on the common was not an absolute right. Obviously this is what I think we ought to be saying even about how many children we have. . . . I hope we don't get to a point where we *do* have to override it . . . but I don't think we ought to shrink away from considering that as a possibility." Singer's views are not universally applauded within the population control movement but are universally listened to. The future Church will have to respond to and deal with a generation of younger zealots educated by the likes of Peter Singer and eager to reintroduce the concept of "responsible" eugenics into the conversation. As I say, an exciting culture clash!

So, quite clearly, the Catholic Church and faithful Catholics show a certain commitment to the saving of innocent and vulnerable life. It is nothing at all to be ashamed of. Remember, at the time of their activism the anti-slavery fighters of the late eighteenth and nineteenth centuries were regarded as extremists and troublemakers who, according to establishment wisdom, would be better off involving themselves in something that mattered. Not bad company to be in, and to be condemned in.

The Church has always held up a mirror in which society can see reflected some of its uglier aspects and it generally does not like what it sees. Which is why it becomes so angry, not, as it should be, with itself but with the Church. This is particularly noticeable when it comes to issues of personal gratification and of sexuality and especially when issues of artificial contraception, condoms, and the birth control pill are discussed. I guarantee that this subject will be at the centre of future demands for change in Church teaching, from inside as well as outside of the Church, and is one that will require careful and resolute formation and understanding to hold the ground.

The Church warned in the 1960s that far from creating a more peaceful, content, and sexually fulfilled society, the universal availability of the Pill and condoms would lead to the direct opposite. In the decades since, we have witnessed a seemingly inexorable increase in sexually transmitted diseases, so-called unwanted pregnancies, sexuality-related depression, divorce, family breakdown, pornography addiction, and general unhappiness in the field of sexual relationships. The Church's argument was that far from liberating women, contraception would enable and empower men and reduce the value and dignity of sexuality to the point of transforming what should be a loving and profound act into a mere exchange of bodily fluids. The expunging from the sexual act of the possibility of procreation, the Church said, would reduce sexuality to mere self-gratification. Pleasure was vital and God-given but there was also a purpose, a glorious purpose, to sex that went far beyond the merely instant and ultimately selfish. The central document in outlining all this was entitled *Humanae Vitae*, both the culmination of generations of Catholic thinking on the issue and a response to the emerging permissive culture. Author

Mary Eberstadt puts the context for this extremely well. "That *Humanae Vitae* and related Catholic teachings about sexual morality are laughingstocks in all the best places is not exactly news. Even in the benighted precincts of believers, where information from the outside world is known to travel exceedingly slowly, everybody grasps that this is one doctrine the world loves to hate. During Benedict xvi's April visit to the United States, hardly a story in the secular press failed to mention the teachings of *Humanae Vitae*, usually alongside adjectives like 'divisive' and 'controversial' and 'outdated.' In fact, if there's anything on earth that unites the Church's adversaries—all of them except for the Muslims, anyway—the teaching against contraception is probably it. To many people, both today and when the encyclical was promulgated on July 25, 1968, the notion simply defies understanding. Consenting adults, told not to use birth control? Preposterous. Third World parents deprived access to contraception and abortion? Positively criminal. A ban on condoms when there's a risk of contracting AIDS? Beneath contempt."[6]

It is this Papal letter, this subject, this theme, that will be at the core of debate in the future Church and its stance on personal morality and sexuality, and its rethinking if not expunging will be the rallying cry of those who advocate changes in Church teaching regarding sexual attitudes. There is a fascinating and indicative paradox involved here; while there are arguably more important components of Catholic theology and morality, it is contraception that so many Catholics mention when they speak of change and the desire for a new, different Catholic Church. The reasons are obvious, and obviously banal. While Catholics may continue to worship and never give a second thought to, for example, the Immaculate Conception or the perpetual virginity of Mary, their right to use condoms or the contraceptive pill matters to them on a daily basis. Matters to them because it matters to them. They can live with a Catholic doctrine they misunderstand, dislike, even reject, but they want their sex to be available, easy, and without responsibility. Suddenly what the Church teaches becomes a genuine problem. Ah, if only they worried more about their doubts about salvation than their desires for sensuality. It's not so much they disagree with the philosophy behind Church teaching, more that it's extremely challenging and difficult to live according to what the Church demands in its teaching concerning birth control. Well, nobody said Christianity was easy; it might be true, it might be right, but it's not easy.

In Section 21 of the encyclical *Humanae Vitae* Pope Paul stated that "the discipline which is proper to the purity of married couples, far from harming conjugal love, rather confers on it a higher human value. It demands continual effort yet, thanks to its beneficent influence, husband and wife fully develop their personalities, being enriched with spiritual values. Such discipline bestows upon family life fruits of serenity and peace; and facilitates the solution of other problems; it favors attention for one's partner, helps both parties to drive out selfishness, the enemy of true love, and deepens their sense of responsibility." It's a superbly pertinent and perceptive analysis, and breathtakingly accurate. Yet the Catholic approach to contraception is not new, and it's nonsense to assume that because *Humanae Vitae* appeared in 1968 the Church had suddenly and recently developed its teaching on birth control. To purposely and artificially obstruct God's plan for marriage and the creation of life was intrinsically wrong, said the encyclical, but natural family planning was permitted because it still allowed the possibility of God's plan to be fulfilled. The document stated that contraception was "any action which, either in anticipation of the conjugal act or in its accomplishment, or in the development of its natural consequences, proposes, whether as an end or as a means, to render procreation impossible." And "we must once again declare that the direct interruption of the generative process already begun, and, above all, directly willed and procured abortion, even if for therapeutic reasons, are to be absolutely excluded as licit means of regulating birth. Equally to be excluded, as the teaching authority of the Church has frequently declared, is direct sterilization, whether perpetual or temporary, whether of the man or of the woman." This included condoms, the Pill, sterilization, and any other unnatural form of obstructing conception.[7]

Tragically there were, are, and will be people who left and leave the Roman Catholic Church over *Humanae Vitae*, but this says far more about them than it does about the Church. It may sound harsh, but this is not about personal convenience, not a game of theological hide-and-seek, but a test of truth and fidelity. With the excessive promotion of flimsy sexual pleasure, the cult of the orgasm, the future Church will be mocked and condemned to a degree recently thought impossible.

Christian teaching against contraception was, however, entirely standard and not exclusively Catholic until the 1930s – the Anglicans softened their position at the 1930 Lambeth Conference due more to member activism than theological consideration and within seventy years became almost indifferent to Christian-based life teachings – but some evangelical denominations are now reconsidering their former approach to contraception. This is fascinating: the future Catholic Church joined in its teachings by Protestants who on many other issues would never compromise with Catholicism. These particular Protestant churches have seen that apart from any Biblical arguments on the issue, the practical results are surprising but clear.

Rather than the old canard that contraceptives have liberated women, contraceptives have tended to allow men to bring pressure to bear on women, telling girlfriends and partners that there is no chance of pregnancy so there is no reason why she shouldn't have sex with him if – yes, that old one – she really loved him. Rather than giving women more control over their sexuality it's often allowed men to take even more power in the equation. The method of natural family planning advised by the Catholic Church is not the regularly joked about rhythm method – another outdated anti-Catholic cliché – but the Billings Ovulation Method in which women monitor their fertility, as well as their gynaecological health, and listen to the natural cycle and demands of their body. Unlike the Pill it is entirely safe and gives control of a sexual relationship to the woman and not the man. It demands respect for women, for nature, and for the act itself, which by necessity then becomes something other than habitual and commonplace. This method of family responsibility needs to be taught more often in parishes throughout the Catholic world, and the future Church needs to explain not what its critics think it believes but it actually believes about this so personal and delicate an issue.

There is, by the way, increasing medical evidence linking the contraceptive pill to women's medical problems, particularly in the area of breast cancer. It's bewildering how the Catholic Church that objects to the use of the Pill is accused of sexism while multinational drug companies who make a fortune out of a product that has millions of women putting alien chemicals into their bodies for decades, sometimes starting in their early teens, escape censure. The Pill fundamentally changes the way in which the female reproductive system is supposed to work and is often, if not usually, as much if not more for men's pleasure than for women's equality. Yet still it's those nasty Catholics who get it wrong and don't want us to be happy.[8] But it is the contraception issue itself that will be at the centre of debates not only between Catholics and non-Catholics, but within the future Catholic Church itself. Critics argue that because many Catholics – in some countries even the majority of Catholics – do not follow the teachings of the Church in this area and use condoms, the contraceptive pill, and other methods and devices to prevent pregnancy, the Church should give up the fight and change its teaching. It's a strange, intriguing approach; they're going to do it anyway, so we might as well say it's the right thing to do. It may well be that many, perhaps most, Catholics are insufficiently charitable, pray too little, fail to forgive and love. Should, then, the future Church change its teachings on these issues to accommodate Catholics who are not as kind, spiritual, and giving as they are supposed to be?

Humanae Vitae appeared in July 1968, and it took only until September of the same year for something known as the Winnipeg Statement to appear, having been written and agreed upon in the Fort Garry Hotel in Winnipeg, Manitoba, in Canada. Its full title was the "Canadian Bishops' Statement on the Encyclical Humanae Vitae," and it not only marked a watershed in modern Catholic history, but is still used by Catholics who advocate not just for a change in teaching on contraception and sexual morals, but on the future place of authority and personal conscience within the Catholic Church. While *Humanae Vitae* stated that contraception is to be "absolutely excluded as a licit means of regulating birth," the Winnipeg Statement says something entirely and dramatically different:

"Counsellors may meet others who, accepting the teaching of the Holy Father, find that because of particular circumstances they are involved in what seems to them a clear conflict of duties, e.g., the reconciling of conjugal love and responsible parenthood with the education of children already born or with the health of the mother. In accord with the accepted principles of moral theology, if these persons have tried sincerely but without success to pursue a line of conduct in keeping with the given directives, they may be safely assured that, whoever honestly chooses that course which seems right to him does so in good conscience." It is truly difficult to overestimate the significance of this declaration, even though it was issued in only one country, with a population then of less than 21 million, with perhaps 8 million of them Catholic. For all that, this was an official document issued by the bishops of the Church. Monsignor Vincent Foy, a champion of Papal teaching, orthodox theology, and Catholic morality and sexual conduct, wrote extensively about the Winnipeg Statement, and worked tirelessly for its reversal. He stated:

"A small group, driven by a Liberal Imperative, persuaded our Bishops to ratify a document which virtually nullified the encyclical of the Pope. It gave couples a veto over human life which God in His love had refused. Countless persons have been barred from existence, countless others conceived but not born because of that document. Every Canadian Catholic living today suffers directly or indirectly from its effects. This is but an outline sketch of the genesis of what is called The Winnipeg Statement. The Church's teaching against artificial contraception was constant and unchallenged from within until the early sixties of this century. In 1964 the errors of Father Louis Janssens of Belgium, Father Schillebeeckx of Holland and others spread like an AIDS virus through the academic circles of many countries, including Canada. . . . In the main, faithful Catholics remained silent. They did not believe their shepherds would turn into sheep and scatter before the theological and 'intellectual' wolves. So the curtain was set to rise on a Canadian tragedy. If we had known the extent of the moral havoc to be launched by The Winnipeg Statement, I think we would all have been weeping: Bishops, priests and people."

He may be right, and perhaps the Canadian bishops began to think so as well. They appeared to try to distance themselves from the mess with their document called Statement on the Formation of Conscience, and in 2008 issued a pastoral letter called Liberating Potential that gave total support to *Humanae Vitae*. But the statement from Winnipeg cannot be expunged, its sentiments cannot be eliminated, and its wording and spirit will be used with perhaps more vehemence in the years to come than in the past thirty years under Popes John Paul II and Benedict XVI. While the Church relies on the Papacy and the Magisterium to interpret Scripture and the deposit of faith, there are those who would like to change all that. They claim to believe in what they call the "democratization" of the Church, and between the 1960s and early 1980s to a certain extent they were winning their chosen battles. That trend has been reversed, but these forces are all the more aware that the next decade may well be their last chance to reform the Church so as to make it more, if you will, Protestant. They see, perhaps correctly, that one of the vulnerable areas of Church teaching is contraception, not because the Church is wrong or weak or shallow in this aspect of its teaching, but because many Catholics simply find the challenges too great and look for some sort, any sort, of excuse to disobey and justify that disobedience. The Winnipeg Statement provided that gap in the wall, but it would be foolish to think that the ideologues behind it wanted, and want, merely a reform of teaching on birth control. While there may be many good if misled Catholics who think rebellion against Papal teaching on one subject will do little harm, it's not a minor or insignificant issue, and for the hardliners it's merely the first step on a far longer and darker path.

It's interesting that when it comes to the use of condoms in Africa, with the ravaging sweep of AIDS in particular, the Church has been widely criticized for daring to expect the same of Africans as it does of Europeans and North Americans, and assuming that we are all capable of sacrifice and a Catholic approach to sexuality. But it's invariably the same Europeans and North Americans rather than actual Africans who do the criticizing. AIDS had cut its way through Africa for almost two generations before many people in the developed world had even heard of it. It killed poor black people who lived many miles away, and in spite of our boast that we care for the under-privileged, that care is often cosmetic and applicable only to those closest to us. In effect, very few people seemed to care. The Church cared, though, and was in Africa caring for people with AIDS long before the disease was widely known in North America and Europe. Even today almost half of all African people with AIDS are nursed by men and women working for the Roman Catholic Church. A Church, by the way, that has also called for all African debt to be forgiven and for a radical redistribution of wealth to be instituted from the northern to the southern hemisphere.

This is seldom if ever mentioned when the Church, Pope Benedict, and now Pope Francis reiterate Church teaching concerning birth control. Nor do critics acknowledge, if they even know, that as a barrier to AIDS and various others STDs, condoms are not particularly effective. Even where AIDS is less of an issue, such as in North America, the increased availability and use of condoms has coincided with an annual increase in STDs and so-called unwanted pregnancies. Just one failure of a condom to work – and in spite of what we are told the failure rate is significant – is not always a mere mistake but can be a virtual death sentence. Condoms enable promiscuity rather than encourage abstinence, and all over Africa, most successfully but not exclusively in Uganda, there are elaborate, empathetic, and extraordinarily successful abstinence programs that emphasize humanity rather than lust.

So the future Church will face misunderstanding, abuse, and anger over its refusal to conform to a sexualized culture that has misplaced love and transformed sex and sexuality into a deity. It won't be the only area of attack, and it's not the first time it has happened. As John Paul II said, "True freedom is not advanced in the permissive society, which confuses freedom with license to do anything whatever and which in the name of freedom proclaims a kind of general amorality. It is a caricature of freedom to claim that people are free to organize their lives with no reference to moral values, and to say that society does not have to ensure the protection and advancement of ethical values. Such an attitude is destructive of freedom and peace." The man who lived through Nazism, Communism, and then Western liberalism certainly understood the context of this struggle and left the Church the template for resistance to what is to come.

EUTHANASIA

WHEN WE SPEAK OF the culture of death, it's imperative to understand that this is not mere hyperbole, not some easy and even misleading rhetoric. True, we no longer face black-uniformed thugs killing with relish, but we do face caring, supposedly loving progressives in white, killing out of concern. This is a major challenge even now and will be a keynote of the battles to be fought by the future Church. Along with abortion, euthanasia is a central ingredient of this murderous recipe. Pope Francis certainly has no doubts as to the severity of it all. "In Argentina there is clandestine euthanasia," he has said. "Social services pay up to a certain point; if you pass it, 'die, you are very old'. Today elderly people are discarded when, in reality, they are the seat of wisdom of the society. The right to life means allowing people to live and not killing, allowing them to grow, to eat, to be educated, to be healed, and to be permitted to die with dignity. In this consumerist, hedonist and narcissistic society, we are accustomed to the idea that there are people that are disposable." He gave tangible, physical proof of that belief when he suddenly appeared at Rome's March for Life, or Marcia per la Vita, in 2013, attended by more than forty thousand people. Because of the large crowds, a sudden Papal appearance is a logistical nightmare for security personnel, but Pope Francis insisted on the highly unusual step of meeting many of the marchers personally. It's genuinely difficult to explain just how empowering and meaningful this was for those men, women, and children on the demonstration who are more used to indifference or downright hostility.

The Catholic Church, however, is explicit and detailed in its approach to euthanasia and makes this abundantly obvious in its catechism. "Those whose lives are diminished or weakened deserve special respect. Sick or handicapped persons should be helped to lead lives as normal as possible. . . . Whatever its motives and means, direct euthanasia consists in putting an end to the lives of handicapped, sick, or dying persons. It is morally unacceptable. Thus an act or omission which, of itself or by intention, causes death in order to eliminate suffering constitutes a murder gravely contrary to the dignity of the human person and to the respect due to the living God, his Creator. The error of judgment into which one can fall in good faith does not change the nature of this murderous act, which must always be forbidden and excluded."

It continues, "Discontinuing medical procedures that are burdensome, dangerous, extraordinary, or disproportionate to the expected outcome can be legitimate; it is the refusal of 'overzealous' treatment. Here one does not will to cause death; one's inability to impede it is merely accepted. The decisions should be made by the patient if he is competent and able or, if not, by those legally entitled to act for the patient, whose reasonable will and legitimate interests must always be respected. . . . Even if death is thought imminent, the ordinary care owed to a sick person cannot be legitimately interrupted. The use of painkillers to alleviate the sufferings of the dying, even at the risk of shortening their days, can be morally in conformity with human dignity if death is not willed as either an end or a means, but only foreseen and tolerated as inevitable Palliative care is a special form of disinterested charity. As such it should be encouraged."

This is not a novel approach but, as with all Catholic moral teachings, is the pattern for the future Church. Forgive the cliché, but it's a matter life and death. That's made abundantly obvious by the fact that more than thirty years ago, in 1980, the Sacred Congregation for the Doctrine of the Faith – once known as the Inquisition but that was long ago and we will let that pass – issued a special Declaration on Euthanasia. The Vatican realized as long ago as the early twentieth century that eugenics would become increasingly influential and that as scientific know-how increased, so would the ability of the social engineers to implement their ideas. The 1980 document declared:

"In order that the question of euthanasia can be properly dealt with, it is first necessary to define the words used. Etymologically speaking, in ancient times euthanasia meant an easy death without severe suffering. Today one no longer thinks of this original meaning of the word, but rather of some intervention of medicine whereby the suffering of sickness or of the final agony are reduced, sometimes also with the danger of suppressing life prematurely. Ultimately, the word euthanasia is used in a more particular sense to mean 'mercy killing,' for the purpose of putting an end to extreme suffering, or saving abnormal babies, the mentally ill or the incurably sick from the prolongation, perhaps for many years, of a miserable life, which could impose too heavy a burden on their families or on society. It is, therefore, necessary to state clearly in what sense the word is used in the present document. By euthanasia is understood an action or an omission which of itself or by intention causes death, in order that all suffering may in this way be eliminated. Euthanasia's terms of reference, therefore, are to be found in the intention of the will and in the methods used. It is necessary to state firmly once more that nothing and no one can in any way permit the killing of an innocent human being, whether a fetus or an embryo, an infant or an adult, an old person, or one suffering from an incurable disease, or a person who is dying. Furthermore, no one is permitted to ask for this act of killing, either for himself or herself or for another person entrusted to his or her care, nor can he or she consent to it, either explicitly or implicitly. Nor can any authority legitimately recommend or permit such an action. For it is a question of the violation of the divine law, an offense against the dignity of the human person, a crime against life, and an attack on humanity. It may happen that, by reason of prolonged and barely tolerable pain, for deeply personal or other reasons, people may be led to believe that they can legitimately ask for death or obtain it for others. Although in these cases the guilt of the individual may be reduced or completely absent, nevertheless the error of judgment into which the conscience falls, perhaps in good faith, does not change the nature of this act of killing, which will always be in itself something to be rejected. The pleas of gravely ill people who sometimes ask for death are not to be understood as implying a true desire for euthanasia; in fact, it is almost always a case of an anguished plea for help and love. What a sick person needs, besides medical care, is love, the human and supernatural warmth with which the sick person can and ought to be surrounded by all those close to him or her, parents and children, doctors and nurses."

As the twenty-first century progresses, we see more organized pressure groups seeking to introduce euthanasia beyond the Netherlands and Belgium, where it is legal, and Albania and Luxembourg, where assisted suicide is legal, and the U.S. states of Oregon, Washington, and Montana, where euthanasia exists in all but name. In Belgium there is even a move to legalize euthanasia for children. It will not happen now, but each time it is discussed and brought before parliament it gains more credibility and support. Remember, Belgium was created in the first half of the nineteenth century as a Catholic state. Future Church, please take note.

Pride hides beneath most that is wrong, from the thinnest of failings to the fattest of crime. The pride that leads us to believe that we, rather than God, are always in control and that our bodies are ours to do with what we want, whenever we want. Sometimes this attitude is invincibly malicious, sometimes almost understandable. When it comes to the subject of euthanasia, we see both aspects of the dilemma. For those promoting what amounts to a cult of death it is horror, pure and simple. For those who are suffering or see their loved ones suffering, the subject is far more complex and delicate. The arguments for euthanasia are perhaps better known than those against it because we hear them publicly articulated on a fairly regular basis. Implicit but perhaps not consciously so in this approach is the notion that disability is somehow a curse, that we have the right and wisdom to make our own decisions about when to die and that so-called mercy killing is administered only after layers of consideration. None of that is true of course, and some of it is positively repugnant. Of course we should strive for a state of affairs where nobody approaching death should experience pain, and experts in the field now know that nobody need do so. All physical pain can be controlled, but insufficient time and money is spent training doctors and nurses in how to deal with end-of-life challenges.[1]

The proposition that a person who feels that they want to die or is making an objective, informed decision about whether to live or die is fatuous. In reality, they are the least qualified people because they are, yes, so terrified and agonized that they want to die. Any of us who has experienced any sort of pain or nausea knows that it is difficult to see beyond the immediate need to be free of distress. Beyond the physical pressures are the emotional ones. The feeling that one doesn't fit in any longer, the attitude that "I've had a good life, the children could do so much with the inheritance I'll leave behind, it costs them so much money to keep me in the home, and I know the grand-children don't like coming all this way to visit me all the time." The media tell them that only the young and sexy matter, they are made to feel by television and radio that life is over by the age of seventeen, there are anti-ageing stores opening on the main street and then we wonder why elderly people feel rejected. A culture that once revered the aged as temples of wisdom now looks on them as slums of irrelevance. The answer is not to help someone die but help them to live.

It is no accident that the people most intimidated by, and active against, euthanasia are the disabled. While we boast equal-ity, we violently discriminate against disability at the earliest opportunity by aborting babies that are considered imperfect and then attempt to pass legislation and create a cultural shift that would make the life of disabled people easier to terminate in their more mature years. In 1993 in Canada, for example, a man called Robert Latimer killed his little girl Tracy. She had cerebral palsy but did not ask to die, was surrounded by people who loved her and even by extraordinary people who were willing to adopt her if her care became too difficult for the Latimers. Mr. Latimer put her in the family car, poisoned her to death with carbon monox-ide, and then put her body into his wife's bed, hoping the girl's mother and the authorities would believe that Tracy had died nat-urally. His crime was discovered and his defence was that he was putting her out of her misery when, of course, he was putting her out of his. When Latimer was arrested and charged and especially after he was imprisoned, media campaigns and petitions sprang up to support him. Almost all the time the defence was at work it hardly ever mentioned the rights of the little girl who had been murdered. It took a child writing in the *Vancouver Sun* newspaper in 1994 to show another side of the issue. "My name is Teague. I am 11 years old and have really severe cerebral palsy. The Latimer case in Saskatchewan has caused me a great deal of unhappiness and worry over the past few weeks. I feel very strongly that all children are valuable and deserve to live full and complete lives. No one should make the decision of another person about whether their life is worth living or not.

"I have a friend who had CP and he decided that life was too hard and too painful. So he really let himself die. I knew he was leaving this world and letting himself dwell in the spiritual world. I told him that I understood that the spiritual world was really compelling, but that life was worth fighting for. I had to fight to live when I was very sick. The doctors said I wouldn't live long, but I knew I had so much to accomplish still.

"I have to fight pain all the time. When I was little life was pain, I couldn't remember no pain. My foster Mom Cara helped me learn to manage and control my pain. Now my life is so full of joy. There isn't time enough in the day for me to learn and experience all I wish to. I have a family and many friends who love me. I have a world of knowledge to discover. I have so much to give.

"I can't walk or talk or feed myself. But I am not 'suffering from cerebral palsy.' I use a wheel chair, but I am not 'confined to a wheelchair.' I have pain, but I do not need to be 'put out of my misery.'

"My body is not my enemy. It is that which allows me to enjoy Mozart, experience Shakespeare, savour a bouillabaisse feast and cuddle my Mom. Life is a precious gift. It belongs to the person to whom it was given. Not to her parents, nor to the state. Tracy's life was hers 'to make of it what she could.' My life is going to be astounding."

So the future Church has to try to take back control of the debate, and in so doing take back control of the language and the frame of vocabulary. We have to be extremely careful, for example, when we use terms like "quality of life" because they are entirely subjective and, anyway, largely without meaning. I see people who are physically and mentally able all the time who have no obvious quality of life. They seem to do no good to or for others; they are selfish, lazy, foolish, rude, and arrogant. Such a life does not seem to be one of any genuine quality. Equally there are millions of people, often living in slum conditions and working in mundane, empty jobs, whose quality of life may be questioned. Or wealthy, privileged but spiritually bankrupt, vacuous men and women who contribute little but take so much. They appear to have no quality of life and thus have no need to be alive. It depends who has the power, does it not, and who is able to make the decisions. In the 1890s and early twentieth century, social engineers and eugenicists advocated an entire systematic program to eliminate those whom they considered to be lacking in quality of life. The anti-Catholic zealot and internationally renowned novelist H.G. Wells wrote of the elimination not only of the mentally and physically ill but of the sexually perverse, the black, brown, and yellow, and anybody who did not "fit in" with the new world of which he dreamed. He was joined in these ambitions by Margaret Sanger, the founder of Planned Parenthood and darling then and now of feminism and abortion rights.[2]

Beyond the intellectually flimsy and morally dangerous definition of "quality of life" there are also semantic difficulties with words such as *terminal*. One of the champions of euthanasia, Jack Kevorkian, when speaking to the National Press Club in Washington, D.C., in 1992, said that a terminal illness was "any disease that curtails life even for a day," and the Hemlock Society, one of the largest and most active pro-euthanasia organizations in the world, frequently uses the word *terminal* as part of the phrase "terminal old age," which has sweeping and terrifying implications. Doctors generally admit that estimates of life expectancy are extremely difficult and dangerous to make, and while informed estimates of life expectancy certainly have a place in medicine there are numerous people every year who live far longer, even years longer, than expected. Sometimes this means a great deal more money is required to keep them alive and keep them well and that means more personal investment from families and more public investment from governments providing institutionalized health care, and from insurance companies providing private insurance. The idea that financial concerns are not taken into account in the realm of euthanasia is naïve in the extreme. Then, of course, we have the slippery slope argument, often dismissed by supporters of euthanasia as being hysterical. Yet some slopes are slippery, very slippery indeed.[3]

Margaret Somerville is a bioethicist of international reputation. In 2010, she wrote, "Although the need for euthanasia to relieve pain and suffering is the justification given, and the one the public accepts in supporting its legalization, research shows that dying people request euthanasia far more frequently because of fear of social isolation and of being a burden on others, than pain. So, should avoiding loneliness or being a burden count as a sufficient justification? Recently, some pro-euthanasia advocates have gone further, arguing that respect for people's rights to autonomy and self-determination means competent adults have a right to die at a time of their choosing, and the state has no right to prevent them from doing so. In other words, if euthanasia were legalized, the state has no right to require a justification for its use by competent, freely consenting adults.

"For example, they believe an elderly couple, where the husband is seriously ill and the wife healthy, should be allowed to carry out their suicide pact. As Ruth von Fuchs, head of the Right to Die Society of Canada, stated, 'Life is not an obligation.' But although Ms. von Fuchs thought the wife should have an unfettered right to assisted suicide, she argued that it would allow her to avoid the suffering, grief, and loneliness associated with losing her husband – that is, she articulated a justification. We can see this same trend toward not requiring a justification – or, at least, nothing more than that's what a competent person over a certain age wants to do – in the Netherlands. Last month, a group of older Dutch academics and politicians launched a petition in support of assisted suicide for the over-70s who 'consider their lives complete' and want to die. They quickly attracted more than 100,000 signatures, far more than needed to get the issue debated in the Dutch parliament. The Netherlands' 30-year experience with euthanasia shows clearly the rapid expansion, in practice, of what is seen as an acceptable justification for euthanasia."[4]

Somerville concluded, "Initially, euthanasia was limited to terminally ill, competent adults, with unrelievable pain and suffering, who repeatedly asked for euthanasia and gave their informed consent to it. Now, none of those requirements necessarily applies, in some cases not even in theory and, in others, not in practice. For instance, parents of severely disabled babies can request euthanasia for them, 12- to 16-year-olds can obtain euthanasia with parental consent, and those over 16 can give their own consent. More than 500 deaths a year, where the adult was incompetent or consent not obtained, result from euthanasia. And late middle-aged men (a group at increased risk for suicide) may be using it as a substitute for suicide. Indeed, one of the people responsible for shepherding through the legislation legalizing euthanasia in the Netherlands recently admitted publicly that doing so had been a serious mistake, because, he said, once legalized, euthanasia cannot be controlled. In other words, justifications for it expand greatly, even to the extent that simply a personal preference 'to be dead' will suffice."

Life is not a sentence but a blessing. Death is guaranteed of course – along with taxes and anti-Catholicism – but to encourage it is a curse. Especially for those who are most vulnerable and do not have access to power, money, friends, and even the basic tools of appeal. The most likely victims of euthanasia are those who are so ill as to have lost the ability to speak, write, and communicate. Father Frank Pavone from Priests for Life sums up their situation and how they should be treated by a civilized society very well. "What about them? That, indeed, is the question for the pro-euthanasia forces. People who cannot communicate are people. This gets to the heart of the problem. A person's inability to function does not make his life less valuable. People do not become 'vegetables.' Children of God never lose the divine image in which they were made."[5]

Children of God. The Catholic attitude toward all of us, at every stage of life. When Pope John Paul II was approaching death, his once fit, muscular body was bent, broken, and decaying. He had been a robust man who hiked, skied, and played soccer. He had resisted Nazis as well as Communists, helped bring down a Marxist regime that had murdered and incarcerated tens of millions, rejuvenated an entire Church, written books that changed the world, and visited country after country and continent after continent to spread the word of Catholicism. He had been shot some years earlier, had suffered terrible health problems, and now felt the approach of death. Yet in all of his last year, in all of his last moments, he showed the great dignity that is there for all of us as we approach the end of this life's existence. He did not want to die but he was entirely content with death, because for the Catholic death is merely the beginning of the next stage of life. Beauty rather than euthanasia; grace rather than assisted suicide; joy rather than mercy killing.[6]

So the future Church must emphasize a number of points in this argument. First, when the ill person and family are given appropriate support, the demand for euthanasia diminishes and even disappears. Second, there are always alternatives to euthanasia, no matter what the culture tells us. Third, we now have evidence that people are euthanized even when they have not requested to die. This is certain to be even more of a problem in the coming years wherever and whenever euthanasia is legalized; once the process is in place, its abuse or legal exploitation always follows. Fourth, euthanasia enables the use of death and killing for other people with other problems; what was once considered immoral and illegal for all becomes moral and legal for some, then for more. Fifth, imagine how people with chronic illnesses and who require long-term and expensive help would feel when they know that others in similar situations have agreed to euthanasia and saved so much time and money? They would feel a burden, a taker, and a parasite. Sixth, we must not attribute quality and standing to one life over another. A physically beautiful person is not of more value and wealth than a physically unattractive person, or an athlete more important than a person who will never leave a wheelchair. The case of Stephen Hawking comes to mind, but even this is misleading and dangerous: intellectual gifts do not place a person higher on some fictitious ladder of human merit. Seventh, if we legalize euthanasia, we give the doctors the right to kill – in fact we will demand that they kill – for the first time in the history of medicine. It is no coincidence that doctors are some of the most active opponents of euthanasia, fearing the damage it will cause to the profession's morale, but also subsequent legal battles, and the destruction of thousands of years of medical ethics. Eighth, the acceptance of euthanasia leads to an increased acceptance of suicide, particularly in the minds of those contemplating ending their lives. Those considering suicide are by the nature of the situation seldom rational and clear thinking. Any factor, any thought, can tip the balance and lead them to an action that in a more sane and ethical world would never be encouraged.[7]

The future Church will face enormous pressure to bend on this issue, and there are already some Catholics who argue that a "more enlightened" approach is more suitable to the new, scientific age. That new, scientific age is more accurately described as a new, media age, where emotional dramas and manipulative documentaries explain that authentic compassion would allow people the right to end their lives, with the help of experts and professionals. The future Church will once again be condemned as an enemy of progress and enlightenment. But it won't be the first time, and certainly not the last. It was wrong in the past, it is wrong now, wrong in the future. Rather like euthanasia.

IV

CHURCH AND STATE

IN MAY 2013, the Prime Minister of Ireland was invited by Boston College in the United States to deliver its annual commencement statement. This event and the reaction to it went relatively unnoticed in the mainstream and secular media, but was in fact a seminal moment in the history of Ireland, Irish Catholicism, and the American Church, as well as in the relationship between Catholic leaders and ostensibly Catholic politicians, and the likely direction of the future Church and how it treats public figures who deliberately, wilfully, and repeatedly defy Catholic teaching but insist on regarding themselves as being Catholic and desire the Sacramental and political benefits of the same.

Context is vital here. For many centuries since the Reformation, Ireland had been a sanctuary, albeit an oppressed sanctuary, for English-speaking Catholics and Catholicism. Irish Catholics had fuelled English and Scottish Catholicism and been at the epicentre of the Church in the United States. This was the Ireland of valiant Catholics slaughtered by Oliver Cromwell, remaining strong through persecution, famine, exile, and rebellion. The Ireland that after independence, and especially under the administration of Eamon de Valera, was a Roman Catholic state as devout and uniform as anything in Iberia or Latin America. Then, from the 1980s and particularly as the twenty-first century emerged, it became vehemently divided, and many would argue was in the midst of a *kulturkampf*, a culture struggle, with a triumphant secular and modernist government declaring war on Church prestige and standing, and challenging Catholic teaching on life, sexuality, and morality.

Added to this was Boston's position as a large and centrally important Irish Catholic city in the North American diaspora, and Boston College as a Jesuit institution of elite academic training, established in the nineteenth century to rival the Anglo-Saxon, Protestant Ivy League colleges – and for forty years having lost much of its orthodoxy and embraced a liberal, often perversely relativist collection of beliefs. It didn't really come as any surprise when Boston College invited a pro-abortion and arguably anti-Church Irish leader to deliver a prestigious address, but the reaction from Boston's Cardinal, Seán Patrick O'Malley, was not as predictable. He is an orthodox man of course, and a fine and good Catholic priest, but he had assisted at the funeral Mass of Senator Ted Kennedy, an internationally influential politician with a deeply worrying personal record and an execrable public one. He had opposed the Church on most of its moral teaching on life issues, often leading campaigns to introduce and extend abortion, same-sex marriage, and other related subjects. O'Malley led a prayer at the Mass, explaining, "As Archbishop of Boston, I considered it appropriate to represent the Church at this liturgy out of respect for the Senator, his family, those who attended the Mass and all those who were praying for the Senator and his family at this difficult time." On this occasion, however, the reaction was fundamentally different. He said:

"Because the Gospel of Life is the centerpiece of the Church's social doctrine and because we consider abortion a crime against humanity, the Catholic Bishops of the United States have asked that Catholic institutions not honor government officials or politicians who promote abortion with their laws and policies. Recently I learned that the Prime Minister of Ireland, the Hon. Mr. Enda Kenny was slated to receive an honorary degree at Boston College's graduation this year. I am sure that the invitation was made in good faith, long before it came to the attention of the leadership of Boston College that Mr. Kenny is aggressively promoting abortion legislation. The Irish Bishops have responded to that development by affirming the Church's teaching that 'the deliberate decision to deprive an innocent human being of life is always morally wrong' and expressed serious concern that the proposed legislation 'represents a dramatic and morally unacceptable change to Irish law.' Since the university has not withdrawn the invitation and because the Taoiseach has not seen fit to decline, I shall not attend the graduation. It is my ardent hope that Boston College will work to redress the confusion, disappointment and harm caused by not adhering to the Bishops' directives. Although I shall not be present to impart the final benediction, I assure the graduates that they are in my prayers on this important day in their lives, and I pray that their studies will prepare them to be heralds of the Church's Social Gospel and 'men and women for others,' especially for the most vulnerable in our midst."[1]

A very concise and polite response, and one that leads us to consider how the future Church will react to and regard public figures and politicians who not only disregard and ignore Catholic teaching, but aggressively lead others to do the same. Principally will this mean, to be direct and precise, that priests, bishops, archbishops, cardinals, and popes will rebuke and correct such politicians private and publicly, and will they make it clear that they will not be given Communion, the Eucharist, the body and blood of Jesus Christ, while they are in a state of profound sin and have put themselves outside of the Catholic family? Pope Francis directed the bishops of Argentina to govern the Church according to a document that makes clear that Holy Communion should be disallowed to anybody who facilitates abortion, and he and future popes are likely to rule thus and make this teaching absolutely clear to the rest of the Church and to its members. "These are the guidelines we need for this time in history," the then Archbishop Bergoglio wrote to the bishops of Argentina in 2007. He emphasized the use of the Aparecida Document as a framework in a letter to the Argentine Assembly of Bishops. The text of the document's paragraph 436 states: "We should commit ourselves to 'eucharistic coherence', that is, we should be conscious that people cannot receive holy communion and at the same time act or speak against the commandments, in particular when abortion, euthanasia, and other serious crimes against life and family are facilitated. This responsibility applies particularly to legislators, governors, and health professionals."[2]

This time in history indeed, as the Church embarks on a new generation of relationships with politicians, presidents, premiers, and prime ministers, and the new governing classes. Obviously where these people are not Catholic, the future Church can do no more than make its position clear and public, but where they are Catholic the Church of the coming years is likely to be far more outspoken; it will be so because it has not been so in the past, and apart from being questionable moral behaviour and theological teaching, the practical results have been catastrophic.

It's vital to emphasize at this point that this is not about punishment or reprimand, not about scolding but about saving. It is bad enough for an individual to support or enable abortion or same-sex marriage or various actions that are contrary to Catholic teaching, but for a politician to influence millions of people and make possible legions of abortions or to destroy the very meaning of marriage is far worse. The depth of the sin is great, and for a person in such a state of sin to blithely pretend that they are in a fit position to receive Communion is grotesquely harmful to their soul. A Pope, a Bishop, a priest, is acting as a loving shepherd rather than a stern parent when he explains to a politician the dangers of such behaviour, and tries with counsel, prayer, and love to turn that legislator around – for the politician's sake, as well as the sake of so many pre-born children, for family, and for the moral future of a nation-state. But when a politician refuses to listen, there have to be certain Catholic consequences, and one of these must be the acknowledgement that these people have put themselves outside of the Catholic family. The cozy, often disturbing and unseemly, friendship between clergy and prelates and politicians who regularly support legislation encouraging abortion and family breakdown is deeply disturbing. Let's consider the case of the late Ted Kennedy, referred to earlier, an internationally known politician and an internationally known Catholic.

NBC got it predictably wrong when it reported after Kennedy's death: "Sen. Edward Kennedy was raised from birth to cherish his Catholicism, and it became both a source of comfort and conflict throughout his life. The son of the country's most famous Catholic family defied church teachings when he divorced his first wife, then was granted an annulment only after he admitted he wasn't being honest when he promised her he'd be faithful. His most significant and public break with the church came with his support for abortion rights. Yet Kennedy also advocated for signature Catholic causes, such as help for the poor, health care and immigration reform, and opposition to the Iraq war. His faith remained a regular part of his life until it ended this week with a priest at his bedside."[3]

No, no, no! This displays an ignorance of Catholic teaching that would simply not be tolerated if applied to other religions and other issues. Opposition to the Iraq war was not a Catholic doctrine, but merely an extension of a point made at the time of the conflict by Rome that the war in question might not have fulfilled every principle of just war theory – the basis for Catholic teaching on issues of war and conflict. The Church at no time suggested that supporting the war, or even participating in it, placed one's soul in danger or removed someone from the pale of Catholic orthodoxy. Good Lord, there were Catholic priests serving as chaplains within several different allied armies in Iraq, with the official backing of the Church. As for poverty, support for the poor is indeed a Catholic belief, but there are very few if any politicians who advocate against the poor. The difference of opinion concerns the best way to alleviate poverty and help poor people, and on this the Church has no official teaching. A politician who publicly argued for ignoring or even killing the poor would certainly be in trouble with the Church, but this is hardly likely to be a point of concern; Kennedy's support for abortion, however, most certainly did lead to any number of poor people, people of colour and people on the social margins, aborting their babies, so the idea that he was an example of Catholic advocacy for the impoverished is a profound misreading and misunderstanding of Catholic beliefs and teaching.

Beyond his political stance was his personal behaviour. The death of Mary Jo Kopechne in 1969 while in Kennedy's car poses numerous questions, legal as well as moral, and the senator's attitude toward women and the sanctity of marriage, while perhaps reformed and cleansed as he matured, was severely anti-Catholic for much of his life. This he may have confessed and been contrite about – we have no idea and cannot see into his soul – but he quite evidently never changed his position on abortion and by his behaviour encouraged others to do the same and not change theirs.

"I am an American and a Catholic; I love my country and treasure my faith," Kennedy said. "But I do not assume that my conception of patriotism or policy is invariably correct, or that my convictions about religion should command any greater respect than any other faith in this pluralistic society. I believe there surely is such a thing as truth, but who among us can claim a monopoly on it?" It's a statement devoid of logic and consistency. Nobody was asking Kennedy to proclaim that Catholicism should command any greater respect in society or country, but that Catholicism should command a greater respect in him, because he described himself as a Catholic and insisted on receiving the greatest gift the Catholic Church can bestow, that of the body and blood of Jesus Christ. Russell Shaw, the former spokesman for the U.S. Conference of Catholic Bishops, put it extremely well when he said that Kennedy's defiance of the Church on abortion and gay marriage "reinforced a corrosive belief among Catholics that they can simply ignore teachings they don't agree with." The example of a Ted Kennedy does irreparable harm, and it would take myriad homilies by faithful priests and speeches by serious Catholics to tear at the cloak of dishonesty he created around these issues and the fundamental subject of what is required of a Catholic in good standing.[4]

Journalist and author Robert Royal wrote splendidly and sensitively about all this shortly after the Kennedy funeral: "The Catholic Church in America suffered another grave scandal this weekend. The scandal has nothing to do with his personal sins. I hope he confessed them and was forgiven, as I hope myself to be forgiven. The Church is always generous to sinners who make even the slightest gesture of repentance. In that, she shows that she is not a merely human society bound by certain rules, but the living communion of saints and the presence in this world of the merciful heart of God. The distress – and the scandal – arise from only one thing: the Church's failure to show the slightest reservation about the man who, more than any Catholic and perhaps more than any American political figure, has led the pro-abortion forces in Washington. Even worse, his longstanding pro-abortion leadership gave political cover to other Catholic politicians and confused simple lay people."

This, continued Royal, is what theological scandal does. It leads other Catholics to go astray because they assume the example set by the famous and powerful is the correct one.

"They might with justification believe that you can be a notorious pro-abortion Catholic and still be publicly honored by the Catholic Church. No one mentioned the issue, let alone took steps to make it clear that the Church means business about life. Some have argued that now is not the time to criticize Edward Kennedy. There will be time enough later. But this is not a matter of criticism. This involves a widespread public misperception of Catholicism – or is it a true perception now? Television coverage of the Mass has spread the image of the Church honoring a well-known Catholic, passionately disrespectful of life. The damage may be irreversible. If you think human respect should govern this moment, *de mortuis* and all that," concluded Royal, "you have a right to your opinion. But the scandal is not about respect towards Ted Kennedy. It's about the Church's own self-respect. As Benedict xvi recently reminded us, real charity exists where we respect truth. Some Catholics have argued Kennedy should have been denied Christian burial. That is wrong, even though he never publicly recanted a grave public sin. But could the Church have commended him to God in a way that paid respect to the 50 million aborted souls who were not here to watch the spectacle?"[5]

The future Church has to come to grips with this challenge, whether it applies to a Ted Kennedy, a Joe Biden, or a Nancy Pelosi in the United States, or a Tony Blair in Britain, or former Canadian prime minister Paul Martin. Blair became a Roman Catholic after he left office but was revealed to have been attending Mass while he was British prime minister with his Catholic wife, who was herself a prominent promoter of contraceptives and artificial birth control. He was known to have received Communion long before he was Catholic, and it is difficult to believe that the priest who gave him the Eucharist did not realize that perhaps the most famous man in the country was not a member of the Church. His administrations were fiercely anti-Catholic, and he has never publicly declared that any of his or his government's actions in this area were wrong. Paul Martin led Canada when it introduced same-sex marriage, the first English-speaking country to do so, even though there was limited popular clamour for the change and it had been rejected time and again by provincial and federal legislatures and most political parties. Martin was a Communicant, boasted of having been an altar boy, and traded politically on his Catholicity. Yet in a speech of quite overwhelming audacity he stated:

"Certainly, many of us in this House, myself included, have a strong faith, and we value that faith and its influence on the decisions we make. But all of us have been elected to serve here as Parliamentarians. And as public legislators, we are responsible for serving all Canadians and protecting the rights of all Canadians. We will be influenced by our faith but we also have an obligation to take the widest perspective – to recognize that one of the great strengths of Canada is its respect for the rights of each and every individual, to understand that we must not shrink from the need to reaffirm the rights and responsibilities of Canadians in an evolving society. Four years ago, I stood in this House and voted to support the traditional definition of marriage. Many of us did. My misgivings about extending the right of civil marriage to same-sex couples were a function of my faith, my perspective on the world around us. But much has changed since that day. We've heard from courts across the country, including the Supreme Court. We've come to the realization that instituting civil unions – adopting a 'separate but equal' approach – would violate the equality provisions of the Charter. We've confirmed that extending the right of civil marriage to gays and lesbians will not in any way infringe on religious freedoms. If we do not step forward, then we step back. If we do not protect a right, then we deny it. Mr. Speaker, together as a nation, together as Canadians, let us step forward."[6]

So according to the prime minister of Canada, the Church was a backwards-looking institution, and there was no contradiction between his Catholic faith and the support for same-sex marriage. It is difficult indeed to believe that this highly intelligent man actually believed what he was saying. He was also supremely naïve – at best – when he claimed that religious people would not face discrimination over their opposition to same-sex marriage, as was made clear in the chapter on same-sex marriage. Indeed, even Catholic bishops in Canada are under attack for their stance. Martin wisely opted to pick and choose the parishes where he attended, aware that there were now clergy who would not offer him the Sacrament of Communion. It is likely that in the future Church people like him will have to pick and choose with far more determination. Pray it is so.

As for Nancy Pelosi, this leading U.S. politician has not only opposed Church teaching for decades, but has aggressively encouraged other people to do the same. In June 2013, she was asked what she thought of a bill to counter late-term abortions, where unborn children have the top of their skulls penetrated and their brains crushed and removed, making it easier for the abortionist to pull their bodies from their mother's womb. Her response was breathtaking. "As a practicing and respectful Catholic, this is sacred ground to me when we talk about this. This shouldn't have anything to do with politics." She is not, of course, a practising or respectful Catholic, but more to the point, it is frightening to contemplate that she sees the questioning of late-term abortions – a sticking point even for those who are pro-abortion – to be somehow sacred. So Catholic teaching is not sacred to her, but the questioning of the mutilation and killing of unborn babies is. Odd, to say the least. Then she delivers the old canard that somehow this has nothing to do with politics. Interesting how ostensibly Catholic politicians routinely reference their religion when they speak of poverty and war, but routinely ignore it and are even angry if it is mentioned when it concerns unborn life and sexuality. In an open letter printed in numerous newspapers and websites, Father Frank Pavone of the organization Priests for Life spoke for many in the Church, and the Church itself, when he said that such a statement made a mockery of the Catholic Church and faith and of the tens of millions of American Catholics who do not support abortion and find it reprehensible. "You speak here of Catholic faith as if it is supposed to hide us from reality instead of lead us to face reality," he said, "as if it is supposed to confuse basic moral truths instead of clarify them, and as if it is supposed to help us escape the hard moral questions of life rather than help us confront them. Whatever Catholic faith you claim to respect and practice, it is not the faith that the Catholic Church teaches. And I speak for countless Catholics when I say that it's time for you to stop speaking as if it were. Abortion is not sacred ground; it is sacrilegious ground. To imagine God giving the slightest approval to an act that dismembers a child he created is offensive to both faith and reason. And to say that a question about the difference between a legal medical procedure and murder should not 'have anything to do with politics' reveals a profound failure to understand your own political responsibilities, which start with the duty to secure the God-given right to life of every citizen."[7]

Pelosi, Martin, Blair, and the likes of Joe Biden and so many others are hypocrites, and the future Church will have less time and more strength when dealing with them. In 2010, Cardinal Raymond Burke, formerly Archbishop of St. Louis and now Prefect of the Supreme Tribunal of the Apostolic Signatura, gave an interview in which he spoke of "the God-centered thinking which has marked the discipline of the church" and then discussed how the Church should deal with politicians and public figures who refuse to even consider the scandal and sin they are causing.

"I think it's only natural to be tempted to discouragement, and I've had those temptations. For instance, on the question of a person who publicly and obstinately espouses the right of a woman to choose to abort the infant in her womb receiving Holy Communion, [it] strikes me as something very clear in the 2,000 years of the church's tradition – she's always firmly held that a person who is publicly and obstinately in grave sin should not approach to receive Holy Communion and, if he or she does, should be denied Holy Communion."

Burke continued that it was essential for the person living in error to be told this, because if they are receiving Communion unworthily they are putting their very souls in danger. Burke admitted that the challenges were difficult and that "it hasn't been easy for me to face this question with a certain number of Catholic politicians. And I've had a number of priests speak to me and tell me how difficult it is when they have individuals in their parish who are in a situation of public and grave sin and so, they look to the bishop for encouragement and inspiration in dealing with this." But, he said, the Church must deliver this absolute truth, "in season and out of season, and whether it's being warmly received or not being received or being resisted or criticized. . . . When a bishop takes appropriate pastoral measures in this regard, he's also helping very much brother bishops, and also the priests."[8]

It's a problem that will face the future Church in a greater degree because the former Church did so little to smother it and put matters right. Many are the politicians who campaign against and vote against Catholic teaching but insist on announcing, particularly at election time, that they are faithful Catholics and that being Catholic sometimes means taking issue with the Church. In fact, they are usually not Catholic, not faithful, and not taking issue. They are exploiting their nominal Catholicism for their own ends. As politicians they can say and do whatever they want, but as Catholics they should speak and act as members of the Church.

When, however, bishops, cardinals, or parish priests rebuke them, the response of the politician and their friends in the media is generally to tell the Church to keep out of politics. Good Lord, reality cries out to be heard. It's not the Church interfering in politics but politicians interfering in the Church. If a politician claims to be a Catholic, a priest has an obligation to guide that person to God and Heaven, and the regular and repeated political support for propositions that contradict Church teaching and Christian belief will take the politician in the opposite direction. It's an act of kindness and not aggression for a clergyman to try to help a politician save his soul, even at the expense of losing his political career. These men and women ought to learn from the lesson of St. Thomas More and his martyrdom due to his refusal to dent Church teaching, his refusal to agree to an end to Papal supremacy and to abandon his support for genuine marriage. One can stand in the man's last dwelling-space – the cell in the Tower of London – and appreciate in the harsh, compellingly beautiful but coldly unforgiving room the contemporary resonance of More's heroism when we compare him as a statesman with those men and women in international politics who claim to be Catholic but work and vote against fundamental Catholic doctrine. They do so with the usual chant that we must separate church and state and that their personal views must not influence their public policies. Which is one of the most disingenuous utterances ever to bruise the body politic.[9]

Truth is not geographical. If it's true in a church or a home, it's true in a parliament or a courtroom. If it's true, it's true. If unborn life is sacred, if marriage can only be between a man and a woman, if unjust war is wrong, if exploitation of the poor and weak is immoral, it's always the case. We would think little of a man who loved his wife when in his home country but was unfaithful to her when on vacation. Or someone who told the truth to one person but an untruth to another. The first is an adulterer, the second a liar. On the abortion and marriage issues in particular it is not that ostensibly Catholic politicians have found the matters complex but that they have found them inconvenient. But if it's a life or a Sacrament it's not trivial, it's not a fashion statement, it's not something mutable and passing, like a party platform position. If they're genuinely Catholic they should be ashamed, if they're just cultural Catholics they should have the courage to admit the truth. What so much of it all comes down to, of course, are men and women not living out their Catholic faith. They also failed during Thomas More's era, when legions of politicians, priests, prelates and people gave in and gave up. That was for the sake of their lives. Today politicians do the same for the sake of their limousines. It would be easier to take if they just told us that their careers were in danger if they voted for the Catholic rather than the party line. Instead they obfuscate with arguments about church and state separation and representing all and not just some of their constituents, supporters, and voters. Nonsense. It's long been established that an elected politician is not a mere delegate and is elected to guide as well as represent. On the subject of the death penalty, for example, it may well be that the majority of the elected official's voters support capital punishment but few of these officials would then feel obliged to vote for hanging. This is about pleasing media rather than listening to the masses.

When it comes to the separation of church and state, this is an American concept that doesn't apply to every country and anyway concerns the protection of the freedom of individual Christians rather than the threat of the interference of Christian ethics into national politics. Anybody who does not understand that does not understand the history of Protestant ministers or Catholic priests and nuns building public hospitals and establishing free education. William Wilberforce and his Clapham Sect, the leaders of the revolt against the slave trade in Britain and its empire, were Christians whose only motivation to end slavery was their Christian faith. Perhaps they, or Martin Luther

King, should have remembered that church and state are entirely separate entities. But for future Catholics and the future Church it is Saint Thomas More who must be the model. A statesman who stood for conscience, who loved life, was not physically brave, and had so much for which to live. But he had more for which to die. Truth and the Church. It is as important now as it was in the sixteenth century. And Catholicism is as important now as it ever was and perhaps even more necessary in a world that appears to prefer confusion to clarity and to long for feelings instead of facts. The denial of Communion to politicians, and especially senior politicians, is going to lead to a seminal division and even a partial break in the relationship between the future Church and the future state. It will not be painless, it will lead to any number of accusations against the Church, but it will remind some politicians and many of their followers what the Church is about and what integrity and religious and moral consistency mean in an age that refuses to appreciate and understand either.

V

FEMALE ORDINATION AND MARRIED PRIESTS

AS SOON AS POPE BENEDICT announced his resignation in 2013, there were questions raised about the future of the priesthood and whether the future Church would suddenly ordain women or allow married men to become Catholic clergy. Actually, these are two entirely separate questions, albeit often originating from a similar source and spirit.

Then, within just a few days of Pope Francis being elected, a group of Roman Catholic MPs and members of the House of Lords in Britain wrote a letter asking the new Holy Father to consider permitting bishops in the United Kingdom to ordain married men as priests. The letter was not extreme, and also explained that celibacy should be retained for bishops – as in Eastern forms of Christianity – to show the "continuing high regard we have for those who are able to live a genuinely celibate life," but it seemed disarmingly early for such a letter, and as a consequence entirely lacking in grace and decorum. It did, however, reflect the view of many Catholics, not only in Britain but in much of the Catholic world, especially in western Europe and North America.

"Your Holiness, We write to you as Catholic members of both Houses of the United Kingdom Parliament," the collection of fairly prominent lay Catholics wrote. "First, we would like to warmly congratulate you on your election and assure you of our prayers and of our support as you work for the deep renewal of the Church. We would also like to place one specific request before you. Your two predecessors, Pope John Paul II and Pope Benedict, guided we are sure by the Holy Spirit, generously permitted the ordination of married Anglican clergy as Roman Catholic priests. These men and their families have proved to be a great blessing to our parishes. Based on that very positive experience we would request that, in the same spirit, you permit the ordination of married Catholic men to the priesthood in Great Britain. In recent years we have been saddened by the loss of far too many good priests. If the celibacy rule were relaxed, there would be many others who would seek ordination, bringing great gifts to the priesthood. We recognise that the Church is serious about the New Evangelisation and the need to renew the Christian faith in our secular societies. As such one of our priorities must be to ensure that parishes have priests to administer the sacraments, therefore we believe that allowing married priests is desirable and imperative."[1]

They were far from the first public figures to ask such questions in recent years. In 2010, the newly appointed Bishop of Bruges in Belgium, Jozef De Kesel, questioned celibacy for priests; in 2009, Professor Jozef Baniak at Poznand University in Poland found that 54 per cent of Polish priests supported an end to mandatory celibacy. In 2008, Robert Zollitsch, the Archbishop of Freiburg, was elected the new president of the German Bishops' Conference, and he had earlier called for a discussion of celibacy for priests, describing it as a "gift," but not essential. French Archbishop Roland Minnerath also supported the introduction of married priests in his book *To the Burgundians Who Believe in Heaven and to Those Who Don't Believe*, and the list could go on. Some of those who make this argument are, to be candid, on the liberal wing of the Church and see an end to mandatory celibacy as merely the first step in a future Church that will be fundamentally different from the past. Thus, what seem like moderate proposals are little more than disguised runs at giant leaps. But there are also good and faithful Catholics, priests and laity, who while conservative and orthodox on other issues do look to a future Church that will embrace celibacy as an option but not a necessity.

In an interview in 2012, the then Cardinal Bergoglio made his position clear. "In Western Catholicism, some organizations are pushing for more discussion about the issue. For now, the discipline of celibacy stands firm. Some say, with a certain pragmatism, that we are losing manpower. If, hypothetically, Western Catholicism were to review the issue of celibacy, I think it would do so for cultural reasons (as in the East), not so much as a universal option. For the moment, I am in favor of maintaining celibacy, with all its pros and cons, because we have ten centuries of good experiences rather than failures. What happens is that the scandals have an immediate impact. Tradition has weight and validity. Catholic ministers chose celibacy little by little. Up until 1100, some chose it and some did not. After, the East followed the tradition of non-celibacy as personal choice, while the West went the opposite way. It is a matter of discipline, not of faith. It can change. Personally, it never crossed my mind to marry. But there are cases. Look at the case of the Paraguayan President Fernando Lugo. He's a brilliant guy. But as a bishop, he had a fall and resigned from the diocese. This decision was honest. Sometimes we see priests fall into this."[2]

The subject is complex and demands some background discussion. We know, for example, that Peter was married but also that he, and other married men who became priests in the early church, began a new celibate life after ordination. Church Fathers in the first four centuries after Christ such as Eusibius, Augustine, Tertullian, Origen, St. Cyril of Jerusalem, and St. Jerome certainly spoke and wrote against married clergy. St. Epiphanius wrote that the "Holy Church respects the dignity of the priesthood to such a point that she does not admit to the diaconate, the priesthood, or the episcopate, nor even to the subdiaconate, anyone still living in marriage and begetting children."[3]

Certainly in Alexandria, Antioch, and Rome, married priests were not the norm, and while married clergy did occur in less urban regions of Christendom it's important to realize that their behaviour was thought of as being problematic and not approved of. There were virtually no married priests by the third century and this continued for several hundred years. By the ninth century, however, the clergy was in crisis and approaching a state of moral and theological decay. Priests and bishops had begun to marry and have children and were leaving their property – in fact, church property – to their families. There were various attempts in the following century to reform the clergy and restore the former celibacy, until in 1139 the Second Lateran Council imposed celibacy on the clergy. The teaching has remained like this ever since.

So the notion that this was some arbitrary and sinister plot by the Church and one that was suddenly imposed on a previously non-celibate church in early medieval Europe is preposterous. Like so many criticisms of Catholicism, it is made by people without any understanding of the actual history of the Church or of dogma. In most circumstances, a belief is codified and confirmed only when it is challenged, the assumption being that it is so self-evident that unless and until challenged, it would be redundant to declare it.

Nor is the Church's teaching of priestly celibacy somehow non-Biblical. The Church and the Bible will be discussed in greater length later, but it's crucial to appreciate that the Church is based on the Biblical command that Peter and his descendants will guide and guard Christians and that he and the Magisterium, the teaching office of the Church, will interpret Scripture and direct Roman Catholics down the centuries. Christ left us a Pope and a Church and not a Bible. So while the Bible is essential, it is not exclusive in explaining to Christians how they live and believe and cannot be used without the teaching of the Church. In fact, if it is used on its own it takes away our sense of Christian balance and allows us to fall in all sorts of directions. The Catholic argument becomes perfectly circular and thus plain perfect. Scripture tells us not to be guided by the Bible alone but by the Papacy as well as the Bible, thus to believe fully and authentically in the Bible is to be directed by the Pope and the teaching office in their interpretation of the Bible.

The Bible itself does state in Corinthians 7–8 and 32–38 that "it is well for them to remain unmarried as I am. . . . It is well for you to remain as you are. . . . Do not seek a wife. . . . He who refrains from marriage will do better," and Paul writes that celibacy enables us to give "unhindered devotion to the Lord" (1 Cor 7:35). Christ Himself tells us "it is better not to marry. . . . Let anyone accept this who can" (Mt 19:10–12). As with any study of a Biblical text it's important to understand context. For example, when in Timothy and Titus there appears to be an argument that a bishop or deacon should be "the husband of one wife" what is really being discussed is a man remarrying – it's an attempt to try to remove from the priesthood men who are in a second marriage rather than an argument in favour of married clergy. In early Judaism, the priesthood was maintained within various families and passed down from father to son, thus necessitating marriage. But this is the old covenant, and even within this model priests were required to abstain from having sex with their wives during the time they served in the

Temple. Catholics believe that priests fulfil this Temple relationship every day – the Mass and the Eucharist mean they are serving in the Temple every day of their ordained lives.[4]

The Church today does allow some married priests who convert from Anglicanism to serve as priests, and outside of the Latin Rite there are Catholic priests who are married, but this is the exception to the norm. In the Eastern Rite, where priests are allowed to be married, they have to be married before they are ordained. In other words, if they are celibate at the time of ordination they have to remain so. As well as this, no bishops in the Eastern Rite Catholic Churches are allowed to be married.

On a practical level, we sometimes hear that if the Church allowed married priests there would be no crisis in vocations and the seminaries would suddenly be thriving and full. We could also argue, I suppose, that if we allowed unqualified or semi-believing people to become priests we would also increase the numbers in the seminaries, but lowering the standard, bending the rules, or making them up as we go along hardly seems like good theology and sound morality. In those churches where married priests are allowed, there is a terrible shortage of vocations and any number of other problems. Many of these churches, the mainline Protestant denominations, are hemorrhaging members and may cease to exist as genuinely international bodies within half a century or even less. But is there really a vocation problem within the Catholic Church? Not according to the official figures. And, as we've already noted, it's always interesting how while some friends of the Church do sincerely worry about these issues, some of the strongest voices outlining what they see as a vocation catastrophe are those who hope rather than fear that it's a reality.

In 1978, for example, there were fewer than 64,000 seminarians internationally whereas the latest figures are closer to

110,000. In the developing world, the increase is even more impressive. Africa has witnessed an increase in vocations to the priesthood of almost 240 per cent and Asia almost 125 per cent. Even in the United States, the numbers are up by close to 60 per cent from thirty years ago. Obviously, the numbers in western Europe and North America are not what they were in the nineteenth century or even the 1950s and before Vatican II and its consequences, but they are increasing and relatively healthy and the quality of seminarians is arguably higher than ever before.[5]

While married clergy can and do exist in the Church, there are several potential problems and even contradictions. Marriage is a Sacrament and as such is obviously held in extremely high regard, but then the priesthood is also a Sacrament. A priest must be devoted to his parish and parishioners, and a husband must be devoted to his wife and children. As children and family figure so large – in importance as well as numbers – within Catholicism, a man could well find himself raising several children with his wife while also being required to be constantly available to his flock. It is inevitable that one if not both areas of his life and the lives of those around him would suffer. This seems to be supported by the experience of Protestant ministers, even in some of the more faithful and serious denominations. Focus on the Family is one of the most influential evangelical organizations in the United States if not the world, and according to their research some of the most pressing concerns and problems for married clergy are issues of pornography, children, and their sexual relationship with their spouse. Focus's results showed that clergy frequently feel guilty about the lack of time they spend with their families, sometimes leading to depression and family conflict. Within safe, stable societies, all this can be challenging, but when it comes to missionary work in what is often a hostile and unstable environment the situation can be positively dangerous. A priest may put his own life in danger in the mission field, but a married minister with children exposes not only himself but those closest to him to the same threats and, tragically, family massacres have occurred several times.

For a personal testimony of priestly celibacy, one of the most moving accounts was written by Bishop John Jukes of Southwark in England. "I have always enjoyed the company of women. Their way of talking coupled with their physical appearance, have provided fascinating objects of wonder and interest. So you will understand how great was the step I took when I was 28 to freely take a life-long vow to God that I would never marry. I am still keeping this vow that I took under the example and inspiration of St Francis of Assisi because by it I am more closely linked to Jesus Christ, son of Mary of Nazareth and Son of God. Now as I celebrate my 87th birthday I reflect upon celibacy as I have experienced it and how this gift of God has placed me at the service of the Catholic Church and the people of God. . . . I am convinced from my own experience that the gift of life-long celibacy has given me a great advantage in presenting Jesus and His teaching to mankind.

"I served for 38 years in the Tribunal for dealing with claims for nullity of marriage. In all these varied duties and activities, it became increasingly clear to me that the gift of celibacy has been an essential element in my response to the intellectual and emotional challenges arising from the needs of the people seeking my help. I hold that each and every human being is made in the image and likeness of God. While each of us is responsible for our own decisions that will determine our individual eternal destiny, there is under God a shared solidarity between us, so that we are called to aid each other in achieving our fulfillment with God. . . . For me, the commitment to life-long celibacy has proved a constant reminder to me of Jesus Christ who came to our world to give of Himself even to suffering death as an act of loving service of me and fellow sinners in ensuring the achieving of eternal salvation for all. In addition to these rather abstract theological considerations, there are the day-to-day practical elements in my life as a celibate that have shaped the way I live for over fifty years.

"It is suggested by some people that the life of a priest must be lonely. This has not been my experience. I have been blessed with an awareness of the presence in my life of Jesus Christ at my side. When in community life human relations have become a burden, when my efforts to serve the people have been rejected or ineffectual, Jesus has helped by reminding me of the rejection He had to sustain. When I have seen the good news of the Gospel spurned I have turned to Jesus. He has never deserted me. He has led me out of the sorrow of failure to remind me that He has sustained me in my celibacy. So I trust in the mercy and generosity of God, embodied in Jesus Son of God and Son of Mary, that has enabled me to live a celibate life of joy for the 87 years of my dwelling in this creation."[6]

Beautiful, poignant, touching, and heartfelt. In the clamour of change, the preservation of first things, permanent things, holy things becomes all the more vital, albeit always difficult. While many outside of the Church will call for change in this area in the next decade, what is refreshing, although in some ways surprising, is how many younger clergy are determined and absolute in their defence of celibacy. They came into the Church and acted on their vocations not so as to change but so as to fulfil and complete God's call to them. Even those Anglican and Episcopalian priests who have swum and will swim the Tiber and thus become married Catholic clergy tend to have traditional views about celibacy; they see their situations as products of a church – the Church of England and its colonial branches – gone wrong, rather than as an argument against changing the basic requirements for the vast majority of Catholic clergy.

When it comes to the ordination of women, however, the issue is actually far more straightforward. In the final analysis, it is an issue of misplaced humility on the part of those who demand such a change, and a misunderstanding of the genuine meaning of equality by those who tend to obsess about it. On June 23, 2013, *Time* magazine published an interview with former president Jimmy Carter. He has taken up ever more extreme positions on a variety of issues, but as a former president and now a respected and influential elder statesman, his words do carry weight. On the subject of female ordination, this undoubtedly intelligent and thoughtful man gave a surprisingly callow, ahistorical reply. "I think there's a slow, very slow, move around the world to give women equal rights in the eyes of God. What has been the case for many centuries is that the great religions, the major religions, have discriminated against women in a very abusive fashion and set an example for the rest of society to treat women as secondary citizens. In a marriage or in the workplace or wherever, they are discriminated against. And I think the great religions have set the example for that, by ordaining, in effect, that women are not equal to men in the eyes of God. This has been done and still is done by the Catholic Church ever since the third century, when the Catholic Church ordained that a woman cannot be a priest for instance but a man can. A woman can be a nurse or a teacher but she can't be a priest. This is wrong, I think." So the Church is abusive and does not embrace equality. Carter then went on to somewhat disingenuously compare this with the enlightened gender approach taken by Baptists in the United States. He does not, however, explain that he happens to reject much of the Baptists' other theology, and that Baptist churches were in the quite recent past often actively racist and even segregated. The reason the Catholic Church established a black university in New Orleans, for example, was that after slavery was abolished, black people may have been free, but no university would give them an education. Catholics do not ordain women because they follow Scripture, Baptists discriminated against black people because they didn't. Carter is no theologian but speaks for many when he reduces this complex and sensitive issue to modernist chatter.[7]

The Church simply does not have the authority to ordain women – in the past, now, or in the future. It's not a question of what anybody would like or want or even need but an issue of Scripture and the teaching of Christ. This might not be important for non-Catholics but it's pretty much all that is important to those who worship and follow Jesus Christ and are members of His Church, the Catholic Church. It is revealing and relevant, however, that many of those who certainly do not believe in and worship Christ or God and rather despise the Catholic Church suddenly become so concerned and zealous about changing that Church when it comes to the subject of women clergy.

The first and more important fact is that Jesus being born male was not some chance event or an accidental decision. This may seem so obvious and self-evident as to be banal, but it's an essential starting point for the debate, and one that must be remembered in future discussions. Because God has a purpose in everything He does, and within the sacrificial system of ancient Israel and the Jewish people, the Sin offering and Passover Lamb had to be a male without blemish, and since Christ fulfils these sacrifices He had to be a man. The Church is seen in Scripture and tradition as a bride with God as the bridegroom – the roles are there for a reason and out of God's plan for us and for the Church. We don't have to believe in God but if we do we surely have to believe that He knows more about His plan than we do. In Catholicism, the priest acts *in persona Christi* (in the person of Christ) as Jesus celebrates the sacraments for His bride, the Church, through the actions of the male priest. It is not a question of equality but of divinity. Sadly, even tragically, divinity seldom has much to do with the shouts and screams for female ordination.

We have long heard argued that Christ was only observing the cultural norms of His day and that two thousand years later we need to adapt just as we have in many other areas where ideas of what is acceptable have changed. Or to put it another way, Jesus was a prisoner of His age and just didn't get it. Apart from the obvious dangers and sheer silliness of such a relativistic approach, the basic premise is fundamentally flawed. Christ ignored or rejected many social and cultural aspects of his time, which is one of the reasons – though not the main one – that He was opposed by the theological and political establishment. He was not a conformist and had no problem at all with interacting with women, much to the annoyance of many of the religious reactionaries of His time. Indeed not only women but women of dubious reputation and questionable pasts were welcomed into his group, an action that was positively shocking to many of His contemporaries. In numerous other areas, He broke with custom and tradition but chose to observe it as well when it mattered and when it was important and necessary for the plan of salvation to do so – culture and tradition were forced to adapt to Him, not He to them. This is extraordinarily important. Christ ordained only men and chose them as His disciples for precise reasons and not out of some peculiarity or banality of time. If the Church has to reflect only its own era and that era's political and social fashions, we are in all sorts of trouble. What if a future Church existed in a time when women were deprived of their rights? Would this mean that the argument for female ordination was suddenly null and void, and held credibility only in the early twenty-first century? Dangerous indeed.

Jesus was also well acquainted with priestesses, who were common in the religions of the era and His homeland, at least outside of Judaism. If He'd wanted to ordain women, there was no stronger and more qualified candidate than Mary, who is the only other person who could have spoken the words "This is my body. This is my blood" and been literally accurate. Yet He chose specifically and deliberately to ordain only men, while giving women enormously prominent positions in His ministry and teaching. Catholics are frequently criticised because of the prominence and respect given to the Virgin Mary while simultaneously condemned for not giving enough prominence and respect to women. While the Pope is, obviously, the Pope and can only be a man, he is not as honoured within Catholicism as the saints and the doctors of the Church. There are hundreds of female saints, many of them the most important and beloved. There are also three women doctors of the Church. If this is misogyny, then the Catholic Church has a lot of learning to do.

Christ's vision for the place of women in the church both during and after His life on earth is centrally important. It is women who first tell of His resurrection, thus being the first people to spread the ultimate good news. Remember that the same Church that is accused of being opposed to powerful women was the body that accepted the Gospels as we know them with their emphasis on the Virgin Mary, the dignity of women accused by men of immorality and sin, and their role in believing in Christ being alive when others doubted. All hugely significant and world-changing. Why would this be if Catholicism was opposed to female influence? It is not opposed at all but merely obedient to Christ's teaching about everything. And everything includes never excluding women from the very epicentre of the Church while embracing the exclusively male nature of the priesthood.[8]

Another argument, a favourite today and guaranteed to be one in the future, is that it's just not fair that men can have what women cannot. Which is a little like a man complaining that he can't give birth but a woman can, an argument that could only be made by a man who has never stood next to his wife as she delivers their child! Sorry and all that, but men and women are different and gender-bending may work in some areas of life but not in the institution that will take you back to God, the creator of the universe. To loosen and reform the priest-hood to include women would be to destroy the priesthood. If you desire a broken cup you can have it, but the cup is no longer whole or complete and is no longer a cup. Women cannot do things that only men can do just as men cannot do things that only women can do. Nor is gender the only obstacle, as all sorts of men do not qualify for the priesthood, including for the most part those who are married. Or men who are not Catholic, or men who cannot make the sacrifices necessary to be a priest, or men who are considered ill-equipped to be priests. We are all equal in the eyes of God and baptism gives us the same dignity, but we cannot all be clergy. In terms of influence in the Church, women such as St. Bernadette or Mother Teresa have had a far greater impact and significance than most men, and this includes most clergymen who live glorious but often anonymous lives.

But the determination to demand change continues, even if some of it becomes positively theatrical. Excommunicated "female priest" – a self-identification – Janice Sevre-Duszynska has been known to demonstrate in St. Peter's Square, calling on the crowds of visitors to march in favour of female ordination. Her efforts are not very successful: at one point she was apparently detained by the police for causing a disturbance, but a more common reaction is that tourists assume she is part of the local street entertainment. We have no information concerning how much they tip her for the fun. The reason she and other women who boast that they have been ordained have been excommunicated – and this is important – is that they have placed themselves outside the Communion of the Catholic Church. It is not so much a punishment as a consequence. If you, for example, leave a family, live somewhere else, change your name, reject that family's ways and rules, and claim to have set up an alternative family, you cannot blame the head of that family for saying you are not really part of it anymore. These women also tend to have certain repeated characteristics. They are Western, they have financial security, they are extremely liberal on every moral issue, they reject Church teaching on numerous issues, and they are older. "As the cardinals meet for their conclave to elect the new pope, women are being ordained around the world," explained Sevre-Duszynska when the conclave met to elect Pope Francis. "There are already 150 female priests in the world. The people are ready for change." Not quite. Real revolutionaries change the world, these women change their sandals and long skirts. The future Church is ready for change, ready to lead change, but not to change teaching on the "first world problems" of ordination of women, but around real issues of poverty and injustice. Younger women in the Church who are more active tend to be more conservative, which is a constant source of pain for these ageing radicals. Rather sad when one thinks about it.[9]

Because of the fashion for claiming sameness in every occupation, there are all sorts of activists who will claim that the Church adopted all-male clergy late in its history and that the early church ordained women. I suppose it would be nice for these zealots if this were the case but then it would be nice if rainwater were beer and if taxes were paid to us by the government rather than the other way round. Not going to happen. Never did happen. Read the Church Fathers, almost any of the Church Fathers, to understand very quickly that priests have always been men and never women. There were certainly women in the early church who belonged to orders of virgins and widows but these were precursors to modern nuns and had nothing to do with early or later priests.

In 1994, Pope John Paul II declared, "Although the teaching that priestly ordination is to be reserved to men alone has been preserved by the constant and universal Tradition of the Church and firmly taught by the Magisterium in its more recent documents, at the present time in some places it is nonetheless considered still open to debate, or the Church's judgment that women are not to be admitted to ordination is considered to have a merely disciplinary force. Wherefore, in order that all doubt may be removed regarding a matter of great importance, a matter which pertains to the Church's divine constitution itself, in virtue of my ministry of confirming the brethren (cf. Luke 22:32), I declare that the Church has no authority whatsoever to confer priestly ordination on women and that this judgment is to be definitively held by all the Church's faithful."

Some radicals assumed Pope Francis would be somehow different, less Catholic, rather Protestant – sometimes it becomes almost funny – simply because, as we described in the introduction, he washed the feet of women shortly after he was elected. They were to be horribly disappointed. "In the theologically grounded tradition the priesthood passes through man. The woman has another function in Christianity, reflected in the figure of Mary," he wrote. "It is the figure that embraces society, the figure that contains it, the mother of the community. The woman has the gift of maternity, of tenderness; if all these riches are not integrated, a religious community not only transforms into a chauvinist society, but also into one that is austere, hard and hardly sacred. The fact that a woman cannot exercise the priesthood does not make her less than the male." He expanded this approach when he spoke of the nature of feminism, which he described as a unique philosophy, but said it "does not do any favors to those that it claims to represent, for it puts women on the level of a vindictive battle, and a woman is much more than that. The feminist campaign of the '20s achieved what they wanted and it is over, but a constant feminist philosophy does not give women the dignity that they deserve. As a caricature, I would say that it runs the risk of becoming chauvinism with skirts."

So there we have it. A future Church refusing to waste time with the colossal and narcissistic digression of the fantasy of female ordination, and courteously and constructively rejecting the understandable if unnecessary and dangerous request for married clergy. A future Church reforming where required, but maintaining ultimate truths and essential doctrine. Marrying, as it were, truth with tradition and Scripture with faith. An ordination made in Heaven.

VI

PAPACY

JUST A FEW WEEKS AFTER his appointment, Pope Francis appointed a group of eight cardinals to help him in his position. It was clearly an indication of the man's modesty, and a touching admission that the administration and reform of the Vatican could not be undertaken alone. Yet the *Irish Times* saw this as the Papal shape of Catholic things to come and an indication of a new Papacy. "Throughout the general congregations which preceded the conclave that elected Francis last month, many cardinals expressed concern about the current nature of church administration, calling for a greater collegiality and more attention to the needs and priorities of local churches worldwide. Many cardinals expressed alarm at the extent to which the Holy See, as evidenced by the Vatileaks and papal butler scandals, appeared to be consumed with careerism, rivalry, in-fighting and corruption. The fact that there is only one curia cardinal – Italian Giuseppe Bertello, Governor of Vatican City State – on the eight-man panel would suggest that Francis has listened to this criticism. Otherwise, the panel is made up of two cardinals from Latin America, one from North America, one from Australia, one from India, one from Germany and one from the Democratic Republic of Congo."

It's worth spending a few moments analyzing this entirely typical reporting of an event that could be genuinely significant for the future Church. Although the *Irish Times* reported accurately, and not especially unfairly, it missed a central point. What Pope Francis actually did was to acknowledge that the position of

Pope has become incredibly challenging in numerous areas far beyond the spiritual. A modern Pope is an administrator, a media communicator, a works manager, in some ways even a corporate chief. Pope Benedict had just stepped down because his ill health made it impossible for him to continue to fulfil the demand of the Papacy, and his successor was acknowledging that in non-spiritual matters he needed help. This is an essential, vital distinction. In non-spiritual matters. Collegiality is one of those buzz words that we will hear a great deal of in church discussion in coming years, and while it is often used innocuously, it is all too often a euphemism for an attack on Papal authority itself. Those who want radical changes in the future Church are convinced – and probably quite rightly – that this could be achieved only if the Church of the next generation is made more democratic, which means communal, which means liberal. It's not going to happen. Pope Francis may have a different style from others who have occupied the position, but a new style is not the same as a revolutionary and ahistorical understanding of the Papacy. Taking questions from a group of schoolchildren shortly after he announced the appointment of the eight cardinals, he said, "Anyone who wants to be pope doesn't care much for themselves, God doesn't bless them. I didn't want to be pope." As for not living in the Papal apartments, something that had been widely publicized, he said, "It's not just a question of riches but also a personality issue. I need to live among people and if I lived on my own, perhaps a little isolated, it wouldn't do me good." These two responses say so much. Pope Francis believes the position of Pope is sacrificial, given by God not as a blessing but as a challenge, to lead Christ's Church on earth. And he gave up the Papal apartments not because he thinks the Pope is not worthy of them, but because of his own emotional well-being.

Cardinal Pell from Australia is a member of the group of cardinals that has been labelled V8, and he made it clear that "in no sense is it a cabinet, so the Holy Father is not answerable to us. And in no sense are we an executive. It is vitally important that the prerogatives of the Successor to St Peter are preserved. There is no doubt that the present Pope is giving every indication of being a strong man, so that this will be the case. . . .The Holy Father – like all popes – needs access to information, not just through official sources. I sometimes use the example of Field Marshal Montgomery in the war. He had a core of middle-ranking officers who worked with him in Headquarters mostly on motorbikes and cycles."

The place of the Papacy within Catholicism is a crucial dimension of the future Church, and Catholics have to under-stand why the Pope is who he is, and the Papacy is what it is. Without it, and without this understanding, it is simply impos-sible to defend and justify Catholic teaching on other issues. Catholicism embraces Scripture, but also acknowledges that Jesus Christ did not leave us a Bible but left us a Pope and a teach-ing office, the Magisterium. Through the Pope and the teaching authority of the Church, the truth of the Bible is guided and guarded through the ages. Interpretation is not left to individuals but to those given the authority and the ability to interpret by Jesus Christ while He was on earth present here among us. In the New Testament, the names Simon, Peter, or Cephas are men-tioned almost 200 times, while the names of all the other apostles combined are mentioned fewer than 140. Peter is mentioned first in the list of apostles by Matthew "to single him out as the most prominent one of the twelve." Throughout the New Testament, he is considered the leader of Christ's followers, and St. Paul would later spend fifteen days with him as a preparation for his own journeys of conversion. But the most important event for Peter, and for us, was when Christ took him and the other apostles on a journey to, well, change his name.[1]

The place chosen was several days from the central ministry of Christ and His followers, far off in the northern tip of the country. Known in modern Israel as Banias and in the Bible as Caesarea Philippi, this area was remote, out of the way, and also supremely pertinent and important. It's a beautiful spot with a natural forest, a waterfall, and luscious rock formations. It was also considered one of the religious wonders of the ancient world and a pilgrimage site for ancient pagans. It had been used for animal and perhaps human sacrifice, and King Herod had built a temple to Caesar Augustus on top of the huge rock that still dominates the area. At the base of the rock was a deep, dark hole considered to be bottomless and known as the "gates of hell." It was before the pagan temple, before the gates of hell, before the place of sacrifice and ignorance that Christ, speaking in Aramaic, gives Simon or Peter the name Kepha or Rock, being Petra in Greek or Peter in English. The exchange is deeply moving. Jesus asks His friends who people say He is. They reply that all sorts of ideas are circulating. That He is John the Baptist, that He is Elijah, Jeremiah, or one of the other prophets. This is all very flattering but entirely wrong. Jesus is the Messiah, but none of them say this because, while they love and revere Him, they do not recognize the Messiah promised by God in the Old Testament in this man they can see and hear. Christ accepts their reply and then turns to Simon Peter: "But what about you? Who do you say I am?"

Simon Peter does not hesitate. He has heard all the arguments, listened to the legalistic objections to Jesus and the explanations even from followers as to why He cannot be the chosen one. "You are the Anointed One. You are the Messiah. You are the Son of the Living God!" Then, from Jesus, "You are greatly blessed, Simon, Jonah's son, for this was not revealed to you through human means. This was revealed to you personally by my Father in heaven. You have heard all the human reasons why I am not good enough to be the Messiah, and you have rejected them all. Thus my Father has found your soul open to receiving the truth from him, and it is this you have just proclaimed." Jesus continues, "And so I now tell you that you are the Rock. On this rock I will build my Church, and the gates of Hell will not overcome it!" And then, "I will give you the keys of the kingdom of Heaven; whatever you bind on earth will be bound in heaven and whatever you loose on earth will be loosed in heaven."

The reference to the keys is taken from Isaiah and refers to the keys of the steward of the kingdom. The throne of King David, however, had been vacant for almost six hundred years until the angel Gabriel had told Mary – as is recorded in the book of Luke – that her son would be given that Davidic throne, which once belonged to his "father David." Jesus is the new and final King of Israel and He appoints as His steward, as the man with total and complete authority of His Kingdom, His Church, and His followers, Peter who is the Rock. The steward was the King's representative while he was away and until he returned. The office was also successive and unchallenged in Israel among the Jewish people and passed down either by father to son or by appointment. In other words, while the individual holding the office of steward would die, the office itself would continue and would never diminish in authority or meaning. This might seem obscure to us, but Christ was speaking to Jews of the first century in a language and with symbols and metaphors that they would understand and appreciate. History was a living, breathing creature to a people who lived by the Scriptures and knew their history as a guide to their future. They would have known exactly what Jesus was saying and why He was saying it. That, of course, is why He spoke what he did and where He did.[2]

Jesus also uses the image of a shepherd and his sheep. "When they had finished breakfast, Jesus said to Simon Peter, 'Simon, son of John, do you love me more than these?' He said to him, 'Yes, Lord, you know that I love you.' He said to him, 'Feed my lambs.' He then said to him a second time, 'Simon, son of John, do you love me?' He said to him, 'Yes, Lord, you know that I love you.' He said to him, 'Tend my sheep.' He said to him the third time, 'Simon, son of John, do you love me?' Peter was distressed that he had said to him a third time, 'Do you love me?' and he said to him, 'Lord, you know everything; you know that I love you.' (Jesus) said to him, 'Feed my sheep.'" Again, these were not words without meaning and not accidental or incidental references. Christ had a specific purpose in mind: to instruct His followers, who knew that "feed" and "tend" indicated teaching and ruling. Jesus is asking Peter, telling him, to shepherd His flock on earth, to govern the Church that He will leave. Thus it was Peter who would speak on behalf of the apostles, who would stand up at the birth of the Church at Pentecost to lead it, and who would be given the authority to forgive sins before the rest of the apostles. And in one of the most human and compelling passages of the Bible, we see John running faster than Peter and arriving at the empty tomb before him. But then he waits, allowing Peter to enter first and before him. It's an exquisite demonstration of humility, and of acknowledging the first Pope's authority.

That the early Church accepted and acknowledged that Peter was the first Pope, and that his successors possessed the teaching authority of the Church, is documented from the earliest writings. In AD 170 Tatian the Syrian wrote, "Simon Kephas answered and said, 'You are the Messiah, the Son of the living God.' Jesus answered and said unto him, 'Blessed are you, Simon son of Jonah: flesh and blood has not revealed it unto thee, but my Father which is in heaven. And I say unto thee also, that you are Kephas, and on this Rock will I build my Church; and the gates of hades shall not prevail against it." Tetullian forty years later: "Was anything hid from Peter, who was called the Rock, whereon the Church was built; who obtained the keys of the Kingdom of Heaven, and the power of loosing and of binding in heaven and on earth?" St. Clement of Rome, the first apostolic father of the Church: "Be it known to you, my lord, that Simon [Peter], who, for the sake of the true faith, and the most sure foundation of his doctrine, was set apart to be the foundation of the Church, and for this end was by Jesus Himself, with His truthful mouth, named Peter." St. Hippolytus in AD 225: "Peter, the Rock of the Church . . . the Rock of the Faith, whom Christ our Lord called blessed, the teacher of the Church, the first disciple, he who has the Keys of the Kingdom."[3]

These quotations may seem esoteric but they represent the deepest feelings of the early Church, the early Christians, the people who risked and often faced martyrdom for their faith. This was not a version of Christianity but Christianity itself. Origen in the early and mid-third century: "See what the Lord said to Peter, that great foundation of the Church, and most solid Rock, upon which Christ founded the Church." And: "Look at [Peter], the great foundation of the Church, that most solid of rocks, upon whom Christ built the Church. And what does our Lord say to him? 'Oh you of little faith,' he says, 'why do you doubt?'" and "Upon him (Peter), as on the earth, the Church was founded." St. Cyprian in AD 246: "For first to Peter, upon whom He built the Church, and from whom He appointed and showed that unity should spring" and "God is one, and Christ is one, and the Church is one, and the Chair (of Peter) is one, by the Lord's word, upon a Rock." St. Cyril of Jerusalem in AD 363: "Our Lord Jesus Christ then become man, but by the many He was not known. But wishing to teach that which was not known, having assembled His disciples, He asked, 'Who do you say that I the Son of man am?' . . . And all being silent, for it was beyond man to know, Peter, the Foremost of the Apostles, the Chief Herald of the Church, not using language of his own finding, but having his mind enlightened by the Father, says unto Him, 'Thou art the Christ,' and not simply that, but, 'the Son of the living God.' And a blessing follows the speech . . . and upon this Rock I will found my Church. . . .'

"St. Gregory in AD 370, St. Basil in AD 371, St. Epiphanius in AD 385, St. Ambrose of Milan in the same year, St. Asterius and St. John Chrysostom, in AD 387, and St. Jerome in AD 393 all wrote that it was Peter who had been given the keys of the kingdom and the leadership of the Church and that this authority and position was passed to his successors. The great St. Augustine in AD 410: "These miserable wretches, refusing to acknowledge the Rock as Peter and to believe that the Church has received the Keys to the Kingdom of Heaven, have lost these very keys from their own hands" and "Why! a faggot that is cut from the vine retains its shape. But what use is that shape if it is not living from the root? Come, brother, if you wish to be engrafted in the vine. It is grievous when we see you thus lying cut off. Number the bishops from the See of Peter. And, in that order of fathers, see whom succeeded whom. This is the Rock which the proud gates of hades do not conquer. All who rejoice in peace, only judge truly." The Council of Chalcedon in AD 451 ruled that "wherefore the most holy and blessed Leo, archbishop of the great and elder Rome, through us, and through this present most holy synod, together with the thrice blessed and all-glorious Peter the Apostle, who is the rock and foundation of the Catholic Church, and the foundation of the orthodox faith, has stripped him [Dioscorus] of the episcopate."[4]

Peter's place is sometimes denied by critics of Papal supremacy and Catholic theology, who use the example of Paul seeming to challenge him: "But when Cephas came to Antioch, I opposed him to his face, because he stood self-condemned; for until certain people came from James, he used to eat with the Gentiles. But after they came, he drew back and kept himself separate for fear of the circumcision faction. And the other Jews joined him in this hypocrisy, so that even Barnabas was led astray by their hypocrisy. But when I saw that they were not acting consistently with the truth of the gospel, I said to Cephas before them all, 'If you, though a Jew, live like a Gentile and not like a Jew, how can you compel the Gentiles to live like Jews?'" Problem is, this is not a challenge to Peter's authority or his teaching but a criticism of his lifestyle. The man may sometimes fail but the teaching is something entirely different. And so to Papal infallibility. Which does not mean that if the Pope says it is raining it is raining or that if he promises some sporting victory for a favourite team it will happen. On a more serious note, it does not mean that Papal comments and opinions, books and articles, views and sermons are without blemish, even though they are certainly worth regarding because of their source. Papal infallibility is quite specific.

Infallibility does not mean impeccability. Infallibility is a teaching about who the Lord is. He is Christ, who promised that "I will be with you to the end of the ages," and who will never let

His Church fall into fundamental error. This is a teaching about the Holy Spirit in the Catholic Church. The Pope is not perfect and is not supposed or expected to be. There have been weak Popes and bad Popes – but not many actually, and nowhere near as many as is supposed to be the case, but it would be foolish to argue that they have all been brave, pure, and brilliant. Nor is infallibility restricted to the Pope. It also applies to the body of bishops when they teach true doctrine. Critics of the Church often speak of Vatican II or the Second Vatican Council as the great "it's okay now and everything is forgiven," as though all that went before the 1960s was reactionary and wrong and all taught by the Council and all that occurred afterwards light and progressive. Actually the Council didn't change very much at all, has often been misinterpreted and exploited, and anyway was a legitimate gathering of the Church and as such simply another stage in Catholic history. It explained infallibility thus: "Although the individual bishops do not enjoy the prerogative of infallibility, they can nevertheless proclaim Christ's doctrine infallibly. This is so, even when they are dispersed around the world, provided that while maintaining the bond of unity among themselves and with Peter's successor, and while teaching authentically on a matter of faith or morals, they concur in a single viewpoint as the one which must be held conclusively. This authority is even more clearly verified when, gathered together in an ecumenical council, they are teachers and judges of faith and morals for the universal Church. Their definitions must then be adhered to with the submission of faith."[5]

As head of the bishops, the Pope obviously has a particular responsibility to and relationship with the Catholic world. When he makes a statement, there are certain absolute requirements essential for that pronouncement to be considered infallible. It has to be in the realm of faith and morals, and it has to be made while the Pope is speaking ex cathedra, or from the seat of Peter, the first Pope. This is not a literal but a metaphorical throne, and it's important to remember that the Pope speaking ex cathedra is extraordinarily rare. As we've seen above, Christ gave Peter and his spiritual successors the keys of the Church and promised him that when he taught and led as the steward of Christ on earth he would not, could not, commit error. We can dismiss Jesus if we like, but, logically, if we follow Him we ought to take what He said pretty seriously. Those who lived in Peter's time did. They certainly understood infallibility, as did the early Church. What infallibility is not is some idea made up in the nineteenth century for obscure or selfish political reasons, as is often suggested by critics. The Church sometimes proclaims doctrines and defines beliefs at various periods and at certain times but this does not imply that they did not exist beforehand or that they were just made up. Beliefs tend to be codified and outlined only when they're challenged. In other words, something considered self-evident, obvious, and extremely well-known might not be announced because it seems redundant to do so. Christ's divinity, for example, was proclaimed in AD 325 but had been accepted by His followers from His own lifetime. They accepted it to such an extent that they were willing to die for Him and His divinity only weeks after His crucifixion and would continue to be martyred in large numbers for years to come. Some may consider that they died for something that was untrue but the point is not what we think but what they thought, and they thought Christ to be the Messiah and divine. They died not for Jesus the good man, Jesus the philosopher, or Jesus the revolutionary but Jesus the Christ, the Messiah. If they were willing to make the ultimate sacrifice for this belief, it must have been an established belief, hundreds of years before it was officially codified. So the Church proclaiming something does not indicate it was not true before the proclamation, and this applies to all Church teachings, including Papal infallibility.

The doctrine was formally defined in 1870 at the First Vatican Council. Critics have suggested that the Pope was acting politically and to extend his own personal power, that he was some sort of isolated champion of the cause of infallibility and that most of the bishops at the council objected to the proposal. This is pure myth. Hardly any bishops objected to the doctrine – because they knew its origins and its historical and Biblical reality; it would have been a contradiction of their faith, and a denial of their position as bishops, for them to have rejected a founding doctrine of Roman Catholicism. A handful of them did have reservations for various reasons, many of those reasons being non-theological, but a more substantial 20 per cent were quite understandably concerned about the timing of the announcement and thought it might offend non-Catholics and also make life difficult for Catholics living in countries then embracing secularism and an aggressive nationalism. It was partly because of these issues of increasing concern, of course, that it was essential to remind the world of Christ and His Church, and the Pope did indeed have the authority to sometimes speak infallibly – the very nationalism and secularism spreading their influence in the 1860s and 1870s in particular in the emergent, unifying Germany would eventually be one of the major causes of the First World War and later contribute to the rise of Nazism and European fascism.[6]

Almost seventeen hundred years earlier, Irenaeus of Lyons had been challenged by not dissimilar attacks concerning the structure of the Church and had responded with "But since it would be too long to enumerate in such a volume as this the succession of all the churches, we shall confound all those who, in whatever manner, whether through self-satisfaction or vainglory, or through blindness and wicked opinion, assemble other than where it is proper, by pointing out here the successions of the bishops of the greatest and most ancient church known to all, founded and organized at Rome by the two most glorious apostles, Peter and Paul, that church which has the tradition and the faith which comes down to us after having been announced to men by the apostles. With that church, because of its superior origin, all the churches must agree, that is, all the faithful in the whole world, and it is in her that the faithful everywhere have maintained the apostolic tradition."[7]

Most of the objections to Papal infallibility, however, are not based on an informed or even uninformed criticism of the history, logic, and consistency of the belief itself but motivated by an opposition simply to what the Pope believes and teaches about a whole collection of controversial issues. The disagreements are actually seldom if ever on issues declared by the Pope when speaking ex cathedra, but infallibility is used to make the Papacy and Church appear absurd or anachronistic.

It's odd that when popes have in recent years declared their concerns about, for example, wars in Iraq, Third World poverty, or the death penalty – all impossible to be matters of faith and morals and ex cathedra – the tired old argument about Papal infallibility is not heard at all. Yet when popes speak about, for example, the rights of the unborn or about the sanctity of marriage, there is always someone around willing to throw in an infallibility reference. This is unquestionably, if not infallibly, true.

A more serious criticism is sometimes heard from non-Catholic Christians who mention the case of Honorius I, a Pope of the early seventh century. The claim is that he believed and, more significantly, taught Monothelitism. This heresy had developed in Syria and Armenia and proposed that Jesus had only one nature, a human nature, as opposed to the orthodox Christian belief that He had two, divine as well as human. The Monophysite heresy had been condemned at the Council of Chalcedon in AD 451. It led to bitter divisions within the Church, as many refused to accept the decision and broke away. In the early seventh century the Emperor Heraclius proposed a compromise, saying that Christ had two natures, but only one will (Monothelitism). In a letter answering a query about this, Pope Honorius seemed to say that there was only one will in Christ. He meant, however, that the human and divine wills of Christ were never in conflict. If there are two natures, there must be two wills. Monothelitism was also condemned as heretical. It strikes at the very heart of Christian belief, and if a Pope had indeed proclaimed this ex cathedra it would have been difficult if not impossible to explain. Catholics believe that under the guidance of the Holy Spirit no Pope could do such a thing, not because he would be reluctant to do so but because he would be unable to do so. The problem for critics of infallibility is that while Honorius may have been one of those bad popes – indecisive, political, opportunistic, unwise – he never made a decision on Monothelitism, let alone declared it a dogma of the Church. The example of weak popes is more an argument in favour of than against infallibility. However flawed they may have been, these bad or unimpressive popes never allowed the Church to teach error and never led Catholics astray. Ignatius of Antioch, as early as AD 110 in his letter to the church in Smyrna, stated: "Wherever the bishop appears, let the people be there; just as wherever Jesus Christ is, there is the Catholic

Church."[8] If we look at this from a more practical standpoint it would have been foolish if not positively cruel for Jesus to have left His followers with no guidance at all but merely a handful of men and women who saw and heard Him, weren't entirely clear on everything He taught, and thought that maybe starting a church and converting the world was a nice idea. It's preposterous. It also insults the notion of Jesus as God and God as loving us and wanting us to be taken care of. The New Testament came along later and was given to Christians by the Church, not by Christians to the Church and not by Jesus to anyone. Christ did not leave anything in writing even though He easily could have. So is it likely that He would have abandoned those He loved so much to the whims and winds of the increasingly hostile world and not left behind someone to teach and guide?

When the anchor is cut loose, the ship wanders and drifts, but then this is what some will hope to achieve in the future Church. Cristina L.H. Traina, a professor at Northwestern University, wrote, "Liberals will want a decentralised, participatory structure that places most power in the hands of national bishops' conferences, in collaboration with the laity. On this view, popes are good for inspiration, pastoral care and ecumenical diplomacy but too far removed from the local details of daily life to rule sensitively on regional questions." While she was arguing as a liberal and in favour of Papal dismantling, she had a point: this is precisely what liberals want. They dislike and fear the Papacy because even popes who have, for example, been more committed to social justice and economic change than to traditional liturgy or conservative worship have remained intensely faithful to their office. If we accept Catholic teaching and Biblical promise, we must also assume that they can do no other. No Pope can teach heresy, and much of what is demanded by modern critics of the Church who remain tenuously within that Church is little more than varnished heresy. Professor Traina wrote her article, by the way, in the *Al Jazeera*.[9]

VII

ECUMENISM AND NEW EVANGELIZATION

THESE ARE TWO VERY DIFFERENT SUBJECTS, and within each of them are various subsections. In the first, ecumenism, we need to look at the future Church's relationship with other Christian denominations, with Judaism, and in particular with Islam. I will not be discussing the Church's relationship with the non-monotheistic faiths such as Hinduism and Buddhism because these will not – I predict – be at the sharp end of the modern Church's challenges with other religions. Evangelization is related to ecumenism, and in some ways another side of the same coin. In this part of the chapter, I will discuss the emerging movements within the future Church, the aspirations and beliefs of young Catholics, and the future of the liturgy. Also, what is known as the new evangelization. But let's begin with ecumenism, and let us not be, well, ecumenical with the truth in this area, particularly when it comes to surely the most pressing aspect of the theme – the future Catholic Church and Islam.

In the early summer of 2013, an ambassador from Sunni Islam's highest seat of learning, the Al-Azhar University in Cairo, suggested that Pope Francis should take "a step forward" in the Church's understanding of the Muslim world by stating publicly that Islam is a religion of peace. "The problems that we had were not with the Vatican but with the former pope," he explained. "Now the doors of Al-Azhar are open. Francis is a new pope. We are expecting a step forward from him. If in one of his addresses he were to declare that Islam is a peaceful religion, that Muslims are not looking for war or violence, that would be progress in itself." But, he added, the new dialogue would not include the other Abrahamic faith, because we "will not take part in any meeting with Israelis." He didn't seem to realize that not all Jewish people are Israeli and clearly failed to grasp that a genuine religion of peace would surely meet with anyone if it could lead to a cessation of conflict. But that was far from the only absurdity in the request, clouded as it was in some *Alice Through the Looking Glass* semantics and double-speak. The former Pope referred to, Pope Benedict XVI, caused frustration and anger in large parts of the house of Islam in September 2006, when at the University of Regensburg in Germany he delivered a lecture entitled "Faith, Reason and the University: Memories and Reflections." Most of the paper was non-controversial and dwelt on the historical and theological differences between Catholicism and Islam. But within the speech, the Pope quoted a fourteenth-century Christian emperor: "Show me just what Muhammad brought that was new and there you will find things only evil and inhuman, such as his command to spread by the sword the faith he preached." Pope Benedict then explained how violence, in the name of any religion or cause, was "incompatible with the nature of God and the nature of the soul."[1]

None of this was new nor was it objectively and rationally speaking shocking and provocative. But as soon as word of it spread in Pakistan, Turkey, the Middle East, Indonesia, and within the Islamic diaspora in Europe there were violent demonstrations, threats, and even calls for the Pope to be killed. Almost certainly to protect the lives and safety of Christians living in majority Muslim countries, Pope Benedict issued an apology, stating, "I am deeply sorry for the reactions in some countries to a few passages of my address at the University of

Regensburg, which were considered offensive to the sensibility of Muslims. These in fact were a quotation from a medieval text, which do not in any way express my personal thought. I hope this serves to appease hearts and to clarify the true meaning of my address, which in its totality was and is an invitation to frank and sincere dialogue, with mutual respect." That he was forced to apologize so as to prevent further violence against fellow Catholics at the hands of Muslims says, of course, much about the elegance and consistency of the original question, even making it rhetorical. Three years after this outlandish, irresponsible reaction from the Muslim world, there was an attempt at restored dialogue, but after 2011 links were largely severed when Pope Benedict dared to call for the protection of Christians in the Arab world in particular after yet another bombing of an Egyptian church, this time in Alexandria.

The litany of attacks on Catholics and other Christians by followers of Islam in Muslim-majority countries is as long as it is bloody. Indeed, I could fill not only this chapter but this entire book with accounts of blasphemy laws, forced conversions, rapes and murders, crucifixions, beatings, kidnappings, as well as church bombings, ethnic cleansing, and the less directly violent but degrading and systematic personal, political, legal, and state discrimination against Christians. What should be established immediately is that the popular version of Arab and Muslim history and the media perception of that history is patently false. Palestine, Syria, and Egypt were at one point almost entirely Christian and represented the very epicentre of Christian thought and energy. By the eighth century, Moslem armies had conquered North Africa and most of Spain and were determined to move into other Christian territory. In the eleventh century, the Seljuk Turks declared war on Asia Minor, modern Turkey, an area that had then been Christian for a thousand years.

It was only after such systematic provocation that in 1095 Pope Urban II called for Europe to take back these Christian lands, mainly because of the screams for help from the eastern emperor in Constantinople. What followed was a number of attempts over more than a century, some successful and some ludicrous, to win back large chunks of the Middle East for Christianity, in an undertaking known today as the Crusades and used inaccurately and unfairly to somehow partly justify or explain Islamic hostility toward Christians.

The last Crusaders were defeated and expelled by 1291, but in their time in the region they had experienced success as well as defeat. The Seljuk Turks were particularly oppressive. They killed unarmed pilgrims, forbade Christian services, and destroyed churches. Moreover, there is no serious doubt that Islam's intention was to move further west and take all of Europe. In the late fifteenth and early sixteenth centuries, Muslim troops forced Rome to be evacuated and also besieged Vienna. Hardly a war of resistance against an alien aggressor.

Nor were the men who took to the Crusades the impoverished thugs we have been led to believe. New research shows them to have generally been wealthy and to have left land and power behind in Europe. Many if not most were also devoutly religious and saw their duty as a pilgrimage. Holy people, however, sometimes commit unholy acts. Once they were in Palestine, Lebanon, and Syria, the battles were conducted like any other military confrontation of the era. That is, with terrible loss of life, enormous suffering but far generally less mass cruelty and sadism than routinely employed by the atheistic military forces of Hitler, Stalin, and their friends. Indeed, the crass statement that "more people have died because of religion than anything else" is bizarre. The officially Godless regimes of the twentieth century alone destroyed that vacuous claim.

Once under Christian control, Jerusalem and the greater Christian kingdom always had a Muslim majority and Muslims were allowed to practise their faith. Nor were there any major attempts to convert them to Christianity. Apart from one brief, non-violent, and largely unsuccessful campaign by the Franciscans, Muslims were seldom the targets of proselytizing. The region returned to Moslem rule and eventually to the Ottoman Turks, who united large parts of the Islamic world and were the most thorough imperialists of the Middle East. It's significant that when critics speak of colonization they forget that there was never really any genuinely European Christian empire in the region. After hundreds of years of Turkish control, the Western powers did conquer the Middle East for a brief period but this was geopolitical imperative rather than religious empire.

Today the Christians of what was once the hub of Christianity and the place of its birth are declining in number and are invariably persecuted. In Egypt, the most influential Arab state, the so-called Arab Spring has unleashed even more anti-Christian bigotry and oppression, and the situation is deteriorating. The future Church will be forced to react in some way – to support the Orthodox Copts, who form the vast majority of Egyptian Christians, but also Egyptian Catholics. Iraq has become brutal and almost intolerable for Christians, Syria is increasingly difficult for local Christians who had for generations been protected by the Assar regime, and in Israel and Palestine there is confusion and ambivalence, with towns such as Nazareth and Bethlehem hemorrhaging young Christian men and women. The Crusades should not have happened. Nor should the Islamic wars of conquest that did so much harm to Christians and Christianity and that provoked and produced the Crusades. A crucial difference is that successive popes have apologized for the wrongs done so many years ago, while both Islamic and atheist fundamentalists say sorry for absolutely nothing.

Much of Islam's war against Christian minorities is, anyway, a long way away from where the Crusaders fought their battles. Pakistan has instituted draconian blasphemy laws, Christians are publicly humiliated and attacked, blamed for crimes and disasters, given the worst jobs, forced to the margins of society. There is discrimination and violence in Turkey, Indonesia, Malaysia, and pretty much anywhere where Christians live as a minority within a greater Islamic culture. So it's hardly a two-way street.

Father Zakaria Botros is a gentle, thoughtful man, one of the leading figures of the Egyptian Coptic Christian community and now obliged to live in exile in the United States after twice being arrested in his homeland and having Muslims in Iran and Saudi Arabia put a $60-million bounty on his head. While he is anonymous to most North Americans and Europeans, Botros is famous or notorious throughout North Africa, the Middle East, and Central Asia, where his daily television broadcasts attract enormous audiences and his website millions of hits. His style is uncompromising. Speaking in Egyptian-accented Arabic and fluent in Islamic scholarship and the various subcultures of the Muslim world, he carefully unwraps the layers of the Koran and the life and teachings of Mohammad and presents his viewers with a virtually unprecedented critique of their faith. It's the combination of accessibility and originality that makes him so threatening to militant Islam. "Look, we know people are leaving Islam because of what I say, and the Muslims know people are leaving Islam because of what I say," he explains. A long pause, then: "People in the West simply don't understand the significance of this in a Muslim world that has not and probably will not embrace pluralism. The Islamic response is not to argue with me but to try to kill me."[2] This is central to any future relationship between Catholicism and Islam. If a Catholic becomes a Muslim, Catholics would pray for that person and surely regret the apostasy. But if a Muslim became a Catholic, the chances are that the convert would be killed for what is seen as a crime in the Islamic world.

Nor is this just the sordid reaction of violent fanatics and terror mobs. In 2008, the Iranian parliament passed the "Islamic Penal Code," whereby any woman who left Islam, usually to become a Christian, would be punished with life in prison and any man with execution. One hundred and ninety-six parliamentarians supported the bill, seven opposed it. The world's reaction, including the United Nations, to that contravention of myriad international laws was screamingly silent. Iran merely institutionalized what is already reality in Egypt, Pakistan, Sudan, Saudi Arabia, and the Gulf states. Even in areas of the Islamic world where Christianity has traditionally been tolerated, conversion is still seen as socially and morally criminal.

Yet the Catholic Church has still reached out to Islam and will continue to do so. "The Church regards with esteem also the Muslims," the Vatican declared in an official outreach document to the world's Muslims. "They adore the one God, living and subsisting in himself; merciful and all-powerful, the Creator of heaven and earth, who has spoken to men; they take pains to submit wholeheartedly to even his inscrutable decrees, just as Abraham, with whom the faith of Islam takes pleasure in linking itself, submitted to God. Though they do not acknowledge Jesus as God, they revere him as a prophet. They also honor

Mary, his virgin Mother; at times they even call on her with devotion. In addition, they await the day of judgment when God will render their deserts to all those who have been raised up from the dead. Finally, they value the moral life and worship God especially through prayer, almsgiving and fasting." The document also explored the historical relationship between the two religions, admitting with magnitude that "over the centuries many quarrels and dissensions have arisen between Christians and Muslims. The sacred Council now pleads with all to forget the past and urges that a sincere effort be made to achieve mutual understanding."[3]

This is hardly evidence of a Church labouring under anti-Islamic prejudice, or to use the modern and contrived misnomer, Islamophobia. The future Church can't afford to bury its head and simply reject dialogue with Islam, but nor can it jettison its most vulnerable members living in the Muslim world. Pope John Paul II met with Muslim leaders several times as he travelled the world and in May 2001 was the first Pope to visit a mosque – the Umayyad Mosque in Damascus. His successor, Pope Benedict, stated on his visit to Turkey, "This human and spiritual unity in our origins and our destiny impels us to seek a common path as we play our part in the quest for fundamental values so characteristic of the people of our time. As men and women of religion, we are challenged by the widespread longing for justice, development, solidarity, freedom, security, peace, defense of life, protection of the environment and of the resources of the earth. This is because we too, while respecting the legitimate autonomy of temporal affairs, have a specific contribution to offer in the search for proper solutions to these pressing questions. Above all, we can offer a credible response to the question that emerges clearly from today's society, even if it is often brushed aside, the question about the meaning and purpose of life, for each individual and for humanity as a whole. We are called to work together, so as to help society to open itself to the transcendent, giving Almighty God his rightful place. The best way forward is via authentic dialogue between Christians and Muslims, based on truth and inspired by a sincere wish to know one another better, respecting differences and recognizing what we have in common. This will lead to an authentic respect for the responsible choices that each person makes, especially those pertaining to fundamental values and to personal religious convictions."

A fundamental, perhaps fundamentalist, difference between Catholicism and Islam, however, and an obstacle to peace between the house of Islam and the future Church is the differing manners in which each religion perceives its place in greater or secular society, but even this statement has to be qualified, in that Islam does not acknowledge the validity of a secular society in which it should exist in the first place. There is simply no concept of the separation of mosque and state within orthodox Islam, so that at best the minority religion, including Christianity, can aspire only to toleration and never complete equality. This is totally contrary to the Catholic notion of church and state and has been so for centuries. So while even a majority Catholic society can welcome Muslims as full and equal citizens, a majority Islamic nation can provide a grudging tolerance in theory, and usually a painful sufferance in reality. This leads to twin solitudes of understanding, or a conversation taking place in two different languages with no convincing or reliable translator.

Islamic authority and Jesuit priest Father Samir Khalil Samir believes that "the essential idea is that dialogue with Islam and with other religions cannot be essentially a theological or religious dialogue, except in the broad terms of moral values; it must instead be a dialogue of cultures and civilizations" and of "the totalizing conception of Islamic religion, which is profoundly different from Christianity."

He continues, "In a closed-door seminar held at Castelgandolfo (September 1–2, 2005), the Pope insisted on and stressed this same idea: the profound diversity between Islam and Christianity. On this occasion, he started from a theological point of view, taking into account the Islamic conception of revelation: the Qu'ran 'descended' upon Mohammad; it is not 'inspired' to Mohammad. For this reason, a Muslim does not think himself authorized to interpret the Qu'ran but is tied to this text, which emerged in Arabia in the seventh century. This brings [us] to the same conclusions as before: The absolute nature of the Qu'ran makes dialogue all the more difficult, because there is very little room for interpretation, if at all."[4]

This is extremely well stated. Because beyond interpretation is criticism, even of a respectful kind. Catholics may not be happy with criticism and even less so when it becomes mockery but for generations have accepted this as a reality of modern, post-Christendom life, and the future Church confidently expects to face ever greater attacks and insults. Such a notion is completely alien and entirely unacceptable to Islam and Muslims, which is why textual criticism of the Koran is not allowed in the Muslim world, and why Muslims in Europe, Australasia, and North America are trying, to greater or lesser extents, to introduce such ideas of blasphemy into what are generally liberal and permissive cultures. Surprising as it may seem, the future Church will be part of that liberal and permissive culture – not in that it defends immoral and irresponsible speech and behaviour, but that as a Church that accepts the enlightenment it acknowledges individual rights and freedoms, including the right to offend.

Another dividing factor is the tale of two laws. Canon law is a legal structure designed to organize the governance of the Church within itself, and the future Church will employ canon law as it has always been used. Sharia law, on the other hand, is a legal code designed not merely to govern Islam internally but to provide a framework for the relationship of the Muslim toward everybody else in society and also governs both private and public life, covering most areas of human behaviour. Before becoming Pope Benedict, Cardinal Ratzinger stated, "The Qu'ran is a total religious law, which regulates the whole of political and social life and insists that the whole order of life be Islamic. Sharia shapes society from beginning to end. In this sense, it can exploit such freedoms as our constitutions give, but it cannot be its final goal to say: Yes, now we too are a body with rights, now we are present [in society] just like the Catholics and the Protestants. In such a situation, [Islam] would not achieve a status consistent with its inner nature; it would be in alienation from itself, which could be resolved only through the total Islamization of society. When for example an Islamic finds himself in a Western society, he can benefit from or exploit certain elements, but he can never identify himself with the non-Muslim citizen, because he does not find himself in a Muslim society."

It is difficult to be optimistic about the future Church and its relationship with Islam. While hundreds of millions of Muslims are offended by an innocuous comment made by a Pope about the nature of their faith, the Islamic world still believes that Christians living in Islamic society are *dhimmis* or "non-slaves," allowed to follow their faith but obliged to pay a special tax known as the *jizya*. They can live as Christians but have to show respect and even reverence to Muslims, gain permission to repair and build churches, and cannot communicate their faith, even inadvertently, to Muslims. While Muslims complain of Christians who broadcast the Gospel into Islamic countries by television and radio, churches are destroyed, Muslim converts to Christianity are persecuted and murdered, and apolitical monks and priests are tortured and slaughtered. The future Church may well find itself as one of three competing ideologies for the soul of the world, the other two being secular liberalism and Islam. It will not be the first time Catholicism and Islam have competed, but the battlefield and the weapons will now be completely different.

The future Church's relationship with Judaism will be totally different, and one lyrical with the music of reconciliation and reform. Not that it has always been this way. Catholic hostility toward the Jewish people in greater or lesser degrees has been documented numerous times, and this is not the place for detailed accounts of medieval attitudes and sins. What should be dealt with immediately and definitively is one of the great contemporary errors of perception and understanding, that has, sadly, shaped many attitudes and is still in danger of causing damage to the future Church and its outreach to the Jewish people. This centres on the Holocaust, the Shoah, the great and obscene watershed in modern Jewish history, specifically the allegation that the Catholic Church did little if anything to aid the Jews at their time of ultimate crisis, and that Pope Pius XII was perhaps even partly to blame for the suffering of the Jews. There is a non-Jewish and entirely exploitative context to this as well, in that opponents of Papal power within the Church want to discredit Papal history and thus the current and future Papacy by arguing that the Pope abandoned his moral authority; they then construe that his successors have to delegate power because of this, and that power is always to be delegated to their liberal friends. So, was Pius silent, was the Church complicit in some monumental indifference, and was the Church on the wrong side during one of the great ethical litmus tests of world history? The latter, by the way, is the genuine issue at play here. The new orthodoxy of the Church is terrifying to the older generation of liberals, and they will use history as a battering ram if they can get away with it.

The truth is somewhat different. Before he became Pope Pius, Cardinal Pacelli drafted the Papal encyclical condemning Nazi racism and had it read from every pulpit. The Vatican used its assets to ransom Jews from the Nazis, ran an elaborate escape route, and hid Jewish families in Castel Gandolfo. All this is confirmed by Jewish experts such as B'nai B'rith's Joseph Lichten. The World Jewish Congress donated a great deal of money to the Vatican in gratitude for its wartime work, and in 1945 Rabbi Herzog of Jerusalem thanked Pope Pius "for his lifesaving efforts on behalf of the Jews during the occupation of Italy." When the Pope died in 1958, Golda Meir, then Israeli Foreign Minister, delivered a eulogy at the United Nations praising the man for his work on behalf of her people. For twenty years, in fact, it was considered a self-evident truth that the Church was a member of the victim class during the Second World War and Pope Pius was mentioned alongside Churchill and Roosevelt as part of a triumvirate of good. It was as late as the 1960s that the cultural architecture began to be restructured around this issue, and it's deeply significant that the attacks on the Pope were largely initiated by the German playwright Rolf Hochhuth, who claimed in his play *The Deputy* that the Vatican had ignored the plight of the Jews. What is seldom mentioned is that

Hochhuth was a renowned anti-Catholic who later championed the infamous Holocaust-denier David Irving.[5]

While it is true that the Pope did not issue an outright attack on the Nazis' treatment of the Jews, one of the main reasons was because the leaders of the Catholic Church in Holland had made just such a public statement condemning Nazi anti-Semitism and protesting the deportation of the Jewish people. In response, the German occupiers had arrested and murdered every Dutch Jewish convert to Catholicism they could find. The group included Edith Stein, who was dragged from her convent to the slaughterhouse of Auschwitz, to be gassed in August 1942. She was later declared a saint by the Church. So, actions have consequences, and the Nazis were hardly some civilized group who would be swayed by moral and intellectual argument.

Hundreds of thousands of Catholic religious and laypeople risked their lives and sometimes gave them to help the Jewish victims of the Nazi pagans. To a very large extent their sacrifices have gone uncelebrated, even ignored. Shamefully much of the criticism of the Church comes from within and from critics who use the issue to vicariously attack orthodoxy and Popes John Paul and Benedict. This was precisely the case with John Cornwell's risible book *Hitler's Pope*. In a scholarly response, Rabbi David Dalin's *The Myth of Hitler's Pope* stated that people are trying to "exploit the tragedy of the Jewish people during the Holocaust to foster their own political agenda of forcing changes on the Catholic Church today." Dalin's work has done much to reverse or at least explain the situation, and he's essential reading for anybody who wants to genuinely understand the reality and the subtext of all this.

We also need to recall the actions of another significant Jewish man, another rabbi. In 1945, the Chief Rabbi of Rome,

Israel Zolli, publicly embraced Roman Catholicism. This extraordinary conversion was partly due to Zolli's admiration for the Pope's sheltering and saving of Italian Jews. Zolli suffered greatly due to his conversion, and his motives have been questioned quite dreadfully by his detractors. But that does not change the truth of the situation.[6]

Truth was also misplaced in 2009 when Pope Benedict was accused of "welcoming back into the Church a Holocaust denying Bishop" and as a consequence "ripping to shreds Catholic-Jewish relations for a generation." Which says a great deal more about media inaccuracy than it does about what in fact happened. What Pope Benedict actually did during what became known as "The Williamson Affair" was to lift the excommunication of four bishops who were illicitly consecrated by the late Archbishop Marcel Lefebvre in 1988. Among them was Richard Williamson, who was and almost certainly still is indeed a Holocaust denier and anti-Semite. But the original excommunication had nothing to do with these bishops' views and neither did the removal of the excommunication. Indeed, a major obstacle to what was a welcome and sensible move was the reputation of Williamson, who hated the Vatican as much as if not more than he disliked Jews. He also, by the way, believes that *The Sound of Music* is a pornographic movie and that no self-respecting person should ever watch it.

The history of the issue dates back to Vatican II in the early 1960s. The council's recommendations were relatively mild but they were almost immediately purposely misinterpreted and abused so as to remove Latin from the Mass, ignore Papal teachings, and attempt to transform the historic Church into a stew of ecumenical and subjective ideologies – this war, by the way, is far from over and will continue to be waged within the future

Church and plague it accordingly. The concerted liberal campaign did enormous damage but a new generation of Catholics who rejected 1960s and 70s relativism and embraced a resurgent orthodoxy, empowered by Popes John Paul II and Benedict XVI, won the day. During the darkest times, however, up to a million traditional Catholics left the Church to worship with the Society of St. Pius X, founded by the French Archbishop Lefebvre.

The vast majority of those who joined were merely conservative Catholics who were understandably disturbed by many of the excesses performed, incorrectly, in the name of Vatican II. Others, though, and many within the leadership, embraced a much more reactionary agenda. Some spoke fondly of collaborationist Vichy France, supported the French National Front, and not only rejected the Second Vatican Council but denied that the Church had the authority to call it. Which was, of course, a paradoxically Protestant approach. Most infamous of all these leaders was Richard Williamson, who went on to give an interview on Swedish TV in which he claimed that there were no Nazi gas chambers and that the "so-called Holocaust" was a myth.

It's partly to isolate this individual and his followers, a small minority within the Society of St. Pius X organization, that the Pope expunged the excommunication. The main reason behind the action was the hope that hundreds of thousands of devout Catholics would return to the mainstream Church. Whether this will happen is even now open to question but Williamson has been ostracized from the Society of Pius X. Yet to concentrate on this man is not only an absurd digression from the real debate but also plays directly into his hands by giving him and his rancid ideas a profile they simply do not deserve. He is, as it were, a legend in his own lunchtime.

Numerous European Cardinals and Archbishops, including in France and Germany, publicly welcomed the Papal announcement while simultaneously restating the self-evident fact that the Holocaust happened; that it was devilish; that Jesus, Mary, and the Holy Family were Jewish; and that to be anti-Semitic is to be anti-Christian. It's not clear what else they could have said or done. There are numerous Catholics who have dreadful beliefs but they cannot be excommunicated merely for being wrong or bad. There are legions of alleged Catholics, even priests, who have taught fundamentally anti-Catholic beliefs and not been excommunicated. It's a complex and often disturbing dynamic but is washed far clearer by the tears of Pope John Paul the Great when he openly wept inside the great synagogue in Rome and spoke of the pain and suffering of the Jewish people and how a new bond of love and common fate had developed. All of his magnificent gestures toward the Jews were shared and supported by Pope Benedict, then Cardinal Ratzinger, and now Pope Francis. Future popes will only strengthen that bond.

This was made abundantly clear when Cardinal Jorge Bergoglio first became Pope. One of his first actions was to send a message to the Chief Rabbi of Rome, Riccardo Di Segni: "I sincerely hope to be able to contribute to the progress that relations between Jews and Catholics have enjoyed since the Second Vatican Council." He invited Rabbi Di Segni to the Papal installation, hoping that this would continue the "spirit of renewed collaboration" with the Jewish people. Abraham H. Foxman, national director of the Anti-Defamation League, has been outspoken in his exposing and condemning of anti-Semitism all of his adult life. He explained how Pope Francis specifically mentioned the Jewish delegation in the audience during the Papal installation and thanked them for attending. The Pope then met with leaders of various non-Catholic groups including Muslim, evangelical, Hindu, Sikh, and eastern Orthodox, but referred directly to the Church's friendship with the Jews: "And now I turn to you distinguished representatives of the Jewish people, to which we are joined in a very special spiritual bond, since, as the Second Vatican Council affirms, the Church of Christ acknowledges that 'the beginnings of her faith and her election are already, according to the divine mystery of salvation, in the Patriarchs, Moses, and the prophets. Thank you for your presence, and I am confident that, with the help of the Almighty, we will be able to continue profitably that fraternal dialogue that the Council advocated and that has actually been accomplished, bringing many fruits, especially in recent decades."[7]

Foxman wrote sensitively and accurately at the time that "in one sense, these words are extraordinary coming from a new pope. But in another sense, Pope Francis' warm outreach to the Jewish people is wholly consistent with the many gestures, words and acts of friendship from his predecessors, Pope Benedict XVI and Pope John Paul II. It is consistent with the positive path of reconciliation taking place between Jews and Catholics since the Second Vatican Council in 1965 approved the declaration called Nostra Aetate. Nostra Aetate (Latin for 'In Our Time') states that Jews remain most dear to God, acknowledges the eternal covenant between God and the Jewish people made at Mt. Sinai, rejects anti-Semitism at any time by anyone as contrary to Christianity and declares that Jews were never collectively cursed by God for the death of Jesus. Francis' outreach to Jews also comes as no surprise for those who had followed his career as Cardinal Bergoglio in Buenos Aires, where he celebrated various Jewish holidays with the Argentine Jewish community, including Chanukah, where he lit a candle on the menorah, attended a

Buenos Aires synagogue for Selichot, a pre-Rosh Hashanah (Jewish New Year) service, as well as a commemoration of Kristallnacht, the wave of violent Nazi attacks against Jews before World War II. He also expressed strong solidarity with Argentina's Jewish community following the deadly 1994 bombing of a Buenos Aires Jewish community center."

The book *On Heaven and Earth: Pope Francis on Faith, Family and the Church in the 21st Century* was written in Spanish and published in 2010, but translated into English – and given its obviously new title – only after the Argentinian Cardinal became Pope. It became a key book in understanding Pope Francis, and what is so pertinent about it with regard to the future Church and the Jewish people is that it was written with the Argentinian biophysicist and rabbi Abraham Skorka. The two men discuss many of the major issues of the day, from capitalism to faith, death to atheism, science to poverty. "With [Rabbi] Skorka I never had to leave my Catholic identity behind, just as he didn't have to ignore his Jewish identity," explained Pope Francis. "Our challenge was to proceed with respect and affection, trying to be above reproach as we walked in the presence of God."

We can characterize the new and future Church's relationship to Judaism quite accurately and poignantly by what occurs in a small Bavarian, intensely Catholic town every decade. And where better than Germany for that new dialogue and conversation to take place? The town is Oberammergau, and there are two explanations as to why it was one of the few places not to be devastated by the plague in the seventeenth century. The first is that in 1633 the residents made a sacred vow that if they were spared they would repay God by performing a Passion Play for as long as the town existed. The second is that the astute Germans who lived in this picturesque settlement at the foot of the Alps posted guards in the area and refused entry to newcomers. The romantic to the prosaic, the theological to the medical. Either way it worked. While most of Europe was losing up to a third of its population, Oberammergau remained healthy.

And ever since they have kept their word – who would be brave enough not to? – and with a handful of exceptions for the odd war the villagers have gathered together to recreate the last days of the life and death of Christ. It's usually performed every ten years, and in 2010, the most recent play, more than half a million people sat for six hours as two thousand actors, all of whom have to have been born in the town or have been resident for at least twenty years, continue the plague-defying and God-thanking tradition. It's a big production and it's a big business – $40 million in tickets and goodness knows how much in sales of books, hats, bags, pictures, carvings and statues.[8]

The actors, though, aren't paid above basic expenses, and they act, sing, and work as though this is personal, this is family. To a large extent it is. It's profoundly moving as an experience, whether in a religious, dramatic, or simply historic context. How could it not be so? The location is The Alps, the history is an unbroken link to the early seventeenth century, and the story is, well, the greatest one ever told. As such there is a glorious juxta-position of simplicity and sophistication – in front of a bucolic backcloth there is the most modern sound equipment and set design. But there's also baggage here. Hitler saw the play twice and praised it for its able presentation of the "the menace of Jewry." Oddly enough he didn't dwell on the peace, love, and for-giveness bits. The Nazis saw it all as peasants doing what peasants do, uncluttered and untainted by urban modernity. When the obese cross-dresser and Luftwaffe chief Hermann Göring heard the word *culture,* he allegedly reached for his gun. When Nazi propagandists heard the word, they reached for the Passion Play. Cheap trips were organized for loyal Germans and the party paid for posters advertising the production. They even tried, unsuccessfully, to impose a new, National Socialist script. So if any one entity epitomizes the new, post-war Germany and Catholic Bavaria at ease with its atavistic guilt and open to admission and contrition, it's the Passion Play. What is at the core and heart of all this is the extraordinary transformation from the Jew as Christ-killer to the Jew as Christ. Indeed, one of the reasons that the play is so long – too long, in fact – is that the latest script goes to such lengths to emphasize the Jewishness of the story and the essentially internal struggle within first-century Judaism between supporters and opponents of Jesus.

If anything, everybody tries just a little too hard. The nasty, avaricious merchants in the temple are hardly mentioned, Jesus is constantly described as a rabbi, the Sanhedrin divide loudly and almost violently over messianic meanings, the crowd that condemns Jesus is also bursting with His followers, and the menorahs are enormous. But cynicism would be a painfully flawed reaction. This has all come about not because of some human rights commission intrusion or the spasm of contrived political correctness but due to a new, organic relationship between Jew and Catholic. It's not as though Catholic Germans don't know about what happened seventy years ago. They're taught it in schools, they're lectured about it by their political leaders, and they're the best financial and moral friend Israel will ever have. Very few Germans complain about this, and in Bavaria in particular the conservative, Catholic right has long embraced philo-Semitism.

The producers of the play began to approach Jewish organizations for advice decades ago, and in this latest rendering there is one particularly moving moment when the actor depicting Jesus recites the first verses of the Shema in perfect Hebrew. This is the central prayer of Judaism – "Hear O Israel, the Lord our God, the Lord is One" – and when spoken by a German Catholic actor in a Bavarian town that once boasted a strong Nazi Party membership, it is chillingly effective. Words spoken by millions of Jews before they were murdered by German soldiers now echoing in the German night and listened to with a tearful respect by everybody on the stage. The history and evolution of a relationship between Jew and German Catholic is crystallized in a single moment.

This new friendship isn't confined to Germany of course, and it's been considered a self-evident truth within post-Holocaust Christianity that the Christ story is essentially a Jewish one. But in the past ten years many liberal Protestants have begun to almost institutionalize anti-Zionism as one of their new sacraments. When religious orthodoxy leaves, political radicalism fills the vacuum. In the United States, Britain, and northern Europe, we've seen a worrying lack of balance from many Anglicans, Presbyterians, and Lutherans. It's not that they have no right to criticize Israel, but it might be nice if they realized that if Christians had acted more like Christians in the first place the Jews of Europe would have been less enthusiastic about building a safe national homeland in the Middle East.

The Roman Catholic Church has not followed this path and has done most things possible to repent for what happened in the past, and there is every indication that the future Church will do the same. Sometimes it's been difficult, and some of the Catholic approaches have not been reciprocated or understood in the way it was hoped. Some of the writings by Jewish authors about the Passion Play, for example, have been so uncompromising as to be unhelpful and even damaging. Professor James Shapiro from Columbia University is a good example with his influential 2001 book *Oberammergau: The Troubling Story of the World's Most Famous Passion Play*. The book dwells on an occasionally ugly past and seems annoyingly reluctant to admit the triumphs of the present. It's as though no reform is good enough, no motivation sufficiently pure. As my friend Rabbi Reuben Pupko in Montreal has it, "Jews can never take yes for an answer."

This liturgical dance around historical injustice and contemporary over-reaction will doubtless continue, but it would be far better choreographed if we could be brutally honest. There is such a thing as Jewish anti-Catholic feeling just as there still is anti-Semitism. But the Jewish people's problem ceased to be Christians' a long time ago and now comes from a very different religion indeed. It's tragic that there are still people who seem to prefer denial and ancient feuds to making that tough leap of understanding about the genuine culture war that is being fought. Oberammergau is a living symbol of hope and reconciliation, not of past wrongs, and to interpret it in any other way is not only dumb but dangerous.

The future Church's relationship with other Christians outside of Catholicism is in some ways paradoxically more complicated and challenging. Jewish, Muslim, or for that matter Hindu, Buddhist, or Sikh can, with all due respect, believe whatever they like, in that they do not claim to be following the teachings and examples of Jesus Christ. Anglicans, Baptists, Presbyterians, Orthodox, and various other Christians most certainly do. Of these, there are broadly three main groups. The eastern Orthodox churches, in Russia, Greece, Serbia, Bulgaria, Egypt, and elsewhere, we will deal with last. The others are the mainline and older Protestant churches, invariably liberal in leadership if not completely in membership, and the evangelical churches. The mainline Protestant churches such as Anglican or Presbyterian vary on their different belief systems – that is part of the problem of course, in that without a central authority and a teaching office each denomination, even each Christian, can decide what to believe – but the general thrust is to ordain women as clergy and often bishops, to be vague on issues of life and sexuality, to ordain either openly gay men and women or be on the road to that end, and to be in differing degrees of accepting standard and historical teaching on the basics of the Christian faith, such as the virgin birth, messianic status of Jesus, the literal resurrection, and so on. Some of these churches contain and even actively encourage ministers who reject the bulk of Christian orthodoxy, while others are in the midst of a conflict, often bitter, between traditional and devout believers, and modernist, relativist followers of something vaguely Christian. These churches are all losing members at a devastating pace, and some of them will exist only in name within fifty years, perhaps far less. I write this not with relish but with sorrow, in that some of the finest Christians I have ever met have been from these traditions, and I can only imagine the pain felt by genuine and loving believers who are still within these denominations.

Where there is maintenance or growth in numbers and enthusiasm is in the evangelical or orthodox wings of churches such as the Anglicans, where in the Third World there are still full churches and examples of energetic leadership. The Anglicans present a particular difficulty, because while there are still many Anglican leaders who have much in common with Rome and the future Church, the Church of England still believes, officially at least, that the Catholic Church never left England, and that the Archbishop of Canterbury is the latest in a line stretching back to the original, Roman Catholic Archbishops of the Canterbury see, and so the Catholic tradition has not been broken. This sets them up in direct rivalry with and contradiction of the Roman Catholic understanding of Christian history. Also, many Anglican clergy have left their church for Roman Catholicism, piecemeal over the years, and now officially under something called the Ordinariate, where Rome welcomes Anglican priests, married or not, sometimes with their congregations, into the Catholic Church. Pope Francis may not be as supportive of this as was his predecessor – but some of what we have been told about his reservations may be a misinterpretation of a single conversation – but the process cannot be reversed.

So, while the future Church will welcome dialogue and meetings, it cannot compromise on Christian fundamentals and will also be aware of some of the hideously anti-Catholic stances adopted by some of these churches. At one time, such bigotry came from a right-wing, often atavistic hatred of Roman influence, based on past struggles in Ireland or Scotland, or even on a healthy if misplaced embrace of Calvinist anti-Catholicism. Today the dislike emanates from a left-wing, liberal rejection of the Church's stand on homosexuality, abortion rights, so-called reproductive freedom, and what is absurdly seen as the Church's opposition to gender equality. The future? Friendship without compromise, listening without agreeing, but ultimately a future Catholic Church of enormous numbers watching with sorrow but resignation the death of mainline Protestant churches across Europe and North America.

The evangelical churches are an entirely different issue, because although they disagree theologically with the Catholic Church over the nature of salvation, the place of Scripture, Papal authority, the Virgin Mary, transubstantiation, and so on, they often share the same platform – literally and figuratively – with the Church on life, sexuality, and the pressing moral issues of the day. This will become even more the case in the years to come. In 1994, a group of leading Catholics and evangelicals published a joint document entitled "Evangelicals and Catholics Together." They spoke unofficially, they were almost all from the United States, and it cannot be said that this declaration led to international systemic changes, but it did articulate an underlying sense that had developed between the two churches.

"As the Second Millennium draws to a close, the Christian mission in world history faces a moment of daunting opportunity and responsibility. If in the merciful and mysterious ways of God the Second Coming is delayed, we enter upon a Third Millennium that could be, in the words of John Paul II, 'a springtime of world missions.' (*Redemptoris Missio*). . . . As we near the Third Millennium, there are approximately 1.7 billion Christians in the world. About a billion of these are Catholics and more than 300 million are Evangelical Protestants. The century now drawing to a close has been the greatest century of missionary expansion in Christian history. We pray and we believe that this expansion has prepared the way for yet greater missionary endeavor in the first century of the Third Millennium.

"The two communities in world Christianity that are most evangelistically assertive and most rapidly growing are Evangelicals and Catholics. In many parts of the world, the relationship between these communities is marked more by conflict than by cooperation, more by animosity than by love, more by suspicion than by trust, more by propaganda and ignorance than by respect for the truth. This is alarmingly the case in Latin America, increasingly the case in Eastern Europe, and too often the case in our own country.

"Without ignoring conflicts between and within other Christian communities, we address ourselves to the relationship between Evangelicals and Catholics, who constitute the growing edge of missionary expansion at present and, most likely, in the century ahead. In doing so, we hope that what we have discovered and resolved may be of help in other situations of conflict, such as that among Orthodox, Evangelicals, and Catholics in Eastern Europe. While we are gratefully aware of ongoing efforts to address tensions among these communities, the shameful reality is that, in many places around the world, the scandal of conflict between Christians obscures the scandal of the cross, thus crippling the one mission of the one Christ."[9]

The piece concluded with "Nearly two thousand years after it began, and nearly five hundred years after the divisions of the Reformation era, the Christian mission to the world is vibrantly alive and assertive. We do not know, we cannot know, what the Lord of history has in store for the Third Millennium. It may be the springtime of world missions and great Christian expansion. It may be the way of the cross marked by persecution and apparent marginalization. In different places and times, it will likely be both. Or it may be that Our Lord will return tomorrow. We do know that his promise is sure, that we are enlisted for the duration, and that we are in this together. We do know that we must affirm and hope and search and contend and witness together, for we belong not to ourselves but to him who has purchased us by the blood of the cross. We do know that this is a time of opportunity – and, if of opportunity, then of responsibility – for Evangelicals and Catholics to be Christians together in a way that helps prepare the world for the coming of him to whom belongs the kingdom, the power, and the glory forever. Amen."

This relationship is about working as one on specific issues, joining together wherever possible, but also acknowledging that there are essential difference between Catholics, now and in the future, and evangelicals. The eastern Orthodox question is more acute, in that for many people the ultimate aim is unification, or some would say reunification. The history of the two churches is deeply troubled, often for geopolitical reasons. What is known as the Great Schism occurred in 1054, when the Byzantine Church split with Roman Catholicism. The details are intricate and layered, but safe to say that as nation-states developed – Catholic Poland and Orthodox Russia, Catholic Croatia and Orthodox Serbia, and so on – the differences of religion became as political and cultural as they were theological. Much of the Orthodox world was submerged under Soviet rule in Russia, Ukraine, and the eastern bloc, and under Islamic domination in the Middle East. For generations there was barely any conversation at all, which is especially ironic because the theological differences between the two churches are often relatively minor. Popes John Paul and Benedict stressed the commonality of the faiths, and as the secular world becomes more aggressive, the future Church will have no practical, and no philosophical, alternative than to strengthen its ties to Orthodoxy.

In 2010, a joint statement of the two churches outlined several key points that needed to be addressed. The first of these was mutual recognition. "The numerous Orthodox Churches and the Catholic Church would have to 'explicitly recognize each other as authentic embodiments of the one Church of Christ, founded on the apostles'." Next came a common confession of faith, or statement of beliefs, and then what is coined "accepted diversity." This would mean that Orthodox and Catholic

Christians would "live in full ecclesial communion with each other without requiring any of the parts to forego its own traditions and practices." After this was Liturgical sharing, where "members of all the Churches in communion would be able to receive the sacraments in the other Churches" and then synodality/conciliarity: "Bishops of all the Churches would be invited to participate fully in any ecumenical councils that might be summoned. Synodality would operate at various levels of ecclesial institutions: local, regional, and worldwide." The document then speaks of mission: "As sister Churches, they would also engage in common efforts to promote the realization of a Christian moral vision in the world." Next is subsidiarity: "Those elected to major episcopal or primatial offices would present themselves to other Church leaders at their level," and finally renewal and reform, so the churches could "commit themselves to continuing Christian renewal and growth together."[10]

It's an ambitious statement, and one that will require enormous work, compromise, and sacrifice. Archimandrite Robert Taft, SJ, has been one of the world's leading scholars in Byzantine liturgical studies for decades, is Professor Emeritus of Oriental Liturgy at the Pontifical Oriental Institute, and is respected and admired in the Orthodox world. He is optimistic, if realistic. Speaking of Pope Francis he says, "Even more interesting from the ecumenical perspective is Francesco's emphasis on his primary title, 'Bishop of Rome.' Because a prelate's title to his primacy comes from his local primatial see, not from some personal or super-imposed ecclesiological distinction. I can't imagine that any of our attentive Orthodox observers have missed that! What it would look like is not a 'reunion' with them 'returning to Rome,' to which they never belonged anyway; nor us being incorporated by them, since we are all ancient apostolic sister churches with a valid episcopate and priesthood and the full panoply of sacraments needed to minister salvation to our respective faithful, as is proclaimed in the renewed Catholic ecclesiology since Vatican II and enshrined in numerous papal documents from Paul VI on, as well as in the wonderful *Catechism of the Catholic Church*. So we just need to restore our broken communion and the rest of the problems you mention can be addressed one by one and resolved by common accord. . . . Part of the problem is that some Orthodox do not instruct their people adequately and update them, so ecumenical progress on the upper level often does not filter down to the ordinary faithful. In addition of course, there is the problem of the bigotry of many of the monastics and others towards anyone who is not Orthodox. On how they square this with what Christianity is supposed to be according to Jesus' explicit teaching in the New Testament, we still await their explanation."[11]

It's a struggle for unity and genuine ecumenism on several fronts. It's important to realize that this is not a secular or political, banal attempt to increase numbers or votes. Unity for the sake of unity is mere triumphalism, an empty, jejune, and meaningless campaign to achieve consensus and agreement on the relatively trivial; a race, if you like, to the bottom.

The future Church is about salvation, not selling. Beyond a relationship with other denominations and religions, however, what of the relationship between the future Church and Catholics? How will the new Church spread its message, communicate its truth, evangelize and convert, and how will it conduct its own worship and praise?

Let's start with a fascinating talk given by Bishop Mark Davies of Shrewsbury in the west of England, and one of that country's most impressive priests. He speaks, as have others, of the "twilight of Christian England," and of course this could apply to any Western nation. But, he says, this twilight is not necessarily "entirely negative." Speaking at the Northern Catholic Conference at Liverpool Hope University, he said that Christianity, let alone Catholicism, will be no more than the belief of a "significant minority" in Britain by the time of the future Church; this is already the case in several European countries, and the trend is inevitable in North America as well. But, said the Bishop, this will mean that Catholics are obliged to strengthen their faith and "dispels any ambiguity and requires of Christians a greater clarity in both teaching and witness."

He continued, "I know many voices may urge us to leave well alone, not to disturb what appears dead in our society. Should we not be realistic and concede that the defence of human life, the identity of marriage and the integrity of the family is all but lost? Should we best remain silent so as not to weaken the Church's increasingly, precarious standing in society? We might, indeed, be tempted to speak only of those concerns which accord with the social consensus around us. Pope Francis, however, shows us a different approach by his startlingly, direct way of speaking and the clear witness of his actions. In the North of England we certainly understand plain speaking! The contemporary world, Pope Francis has shown us, is often more ready to listen and take notice than we as Christians are ready to speak or give witness. Amid the twilight of a Christian England this witness will shine out more clearly."

This is central. Within crisis lies opportunity. The word *evangelization* is used far too often, to the point where repetition has obscured meaning. It has become a qualifying term, garnishing otherwise facile suggestions with a religious importance they do not merit. What we really mean here is how do we deliver Catholic truth to a new generation of people whose concentration is often limited to the sound bite, fed on twenty-four-hour news, instant Internet accessibility, entertainment disguised as information and information posing as entertainment, and a cynicism toward traditional religion that borders on and often crosses into the contemptuous. But let's first deal with Catholics themselves. The truth is that the Church has done a truly awful job in catechizing and forming Catholics for two generations now, and the future Church must deal with this disaster if it is to gain vocations, activists, and simply congregants. Catholic schools and colleges often have tenuous links to anything seriously Catholic, so much so that genuinely Catholic parents often prefer to send their children to secular schools where they will receive no religious education rather than ostensibly Catholic schools where they receive a distorted and bruised religious education.

Canada is a case in point. Catholics sacrificed for decades to send their children to private Catholic schools where they received a fine, faithful education and formation. Catholic parents, teachers, and politicians then worked to achieve public funding for their schools and were successful. They found, however, that Caesar demands payment for what he gives. These schools and their teachers have become sad replicas of what once was. In 2012, the Ontario Catholic English Teachers Association (OECTA) published its annual conference resolutions, and they make for sad, unintentionally amusing but entirely typical reading – they are replicated throughout North America and Europe. As in most Catholic schools, the vast majority of teachers – while often decent and dedicated – are non-practising and even anti-Church. They are divorced, are gay, abort, and use contraceptives, live together, never attend Mass, reject Catholic teaching, are indifferent or even hostile to the religion they are supposed to be part of. Perhaps 20 per cent or so are in some way Catholic in any meaningful sense of the word, and while this might be denied, it is proven by the tiny number of children who leave such schools with any knowledge of and love for the Catholic Church. The minority of principals, teachers, and trustees who defend Catholic moral teaching are attacked not just by leftist politicians, but by other staff and by the unions.

The 2012 OECTA conference resolutions, for example, called on teachers to "endorse and encourage the formation of support groups in keeping with the philosophy and objectives of Gay-Straight Alliances." These "GSAS" are effectively gay support groups, masquerading as anti-bullying networks. They promote total acceptance of homosexuality and resolutely refuse to teach Catholic approaches to the gay person and the gay lifestyle. The resolution continued that support for these GSAS was in keeping with the teaching of the Catholic bishops. That was a downright lie. All rounded off with highly paid and highly anti-Catholic speakers coming in to explain why the Church is out of place and out of touch. This is, I must emphasize, usual, typical, common, and horribly damaging.[12]

Similar tales can be found in London, New York, Paris, Madrid, and Dublin – wherever, in fact, Catholic education has been hijacked by people whose love is for what they would term social justice instead of for the Church, or where secular indifference has drowned out any religiosity or faithfulness. It's a terribly regrettable state of affairs and extends into college and university level. In 2010, a young Catholic woman writing under the pen name of Emmy Cecilia wrote an incisive and brave article about what it was like for a practising Catholic to attend a large, prestigious Catholic university. Her account could have been given by so many other young people who assumed they would be receiving a Catholic education.

"Being at a CINO (Catholic in Name Only) college is hard and getting harder. I'm beginning to see certain assignments marked down. The tension between professors and certain students (myself included) is beginning to increase. My anxiety's also beginning to get a lot worse. . . .

"On Friday I was talking to another faithful Catholic and she was talking about leaving the school as soon as the semester was over . . . and she's not the only one. Many of us who do not agree with the 'teachings' that happen at that school are considering transferring elsewhere, even if it means losing this semester. I had the good fortune of meeting a former student and she said she left after a year because she went through the same that I went through with the professors . . . and she had the same professors, years ago, that I have now. You can just imagine how bad things are. I don't 100% regret going there only because it's taught me a valuable lesson, but I wish I would've really looked at the school before even applying. I knew things were bad but I didn't know the extent of it until I actually got there. I think I can withstand the abuse (and I feel like it is a form of abuse) for another semester or even until I graduate but I am not 100% sure. As I said, my anxiety is getting worse (so much worse) so I am really thinking about what to do."

Her advice to parents and young people was to research Catholic colleges, avoid what she termed CINO colleges, and be extremely careful when applying to what might appear to be Catholic colleges but are in fact centres of anti-Catholicism. She then broke off her article, explaining that she had to write "a 7-page essay on the New Testament . . . which I don't expect to receive full credit on because (like the other assignments) I fail to write what she wants us to write . . . because I don't agree with what she's teaching or her beliefs. That's right, I am purposely refusing to write what she wants us to because I can't, consciously, agree with it. And the professor is supposed to be open minded. Go figure."

It's a heartbreaking story. So what is the future Church to do? The process has already started of establishing a new series of Catholic colleges, because with the best will possible there is simply no possibility of restoring the institutions such as Georgetown, Notre Dame, Fordham, and Boston College in the United States or St. Michael's College in Toronto or St. Jerome's in Waterloo, Ontario, or any number in Europe to anything resembling Catholic education in the authentic sense. The new colleges and universities – Thomas Aquinas College, Christendom College, Ave Maria University in the United States, Our Lady Seat of Wisdom Academy in Canada – are attracting the best, brightest, and most devout of young Catholics, and there are likely to be many more such venues in the future Church. When it comes to younger people as a whole, we need to learn from the phenomenon known as World Youth Day, and from its successes as well as failures. It was started by Pope John Paul II in the mid-1980s, and since then has been held in Argentina, Spain, the United States, Canada, Britain, Germany, Australia, and elsewhere. In the Philippines in 2005, 5 million people gathered, confirmed by the *Guinness Book of Records* as the largest crowd in history. So the suggestion that young people are not interested, that people in general are not interested, is clearly false. What the future Church has to do with the World Youth Days is to follow them up with local initiatives and not allow them to become stand-alone events that appear, amaze, and then disappear. This has happened with several, perhaps most of them.

What we do see is that younger people are attracted to and by orthodoxy. They don't want slightly Catholicized versions of what they encounter on a daily basis, but a glimpse of the beauty and eternal grace of Catholic worship. They want mystery, splendor, the supernatural truth of the Gospels. The reason so many teenagers buy so many vampire novels and people in their twenties read and watch sword and sorcery stories is that they need an alternative, even a flimsy, fatuous alternative, to the increasingly empty reality of modernity. The Church provides the real thing, the concrete foundations rather than the shaky deck. The Catholic truth is there in any Mass, any encounter with the Church, but the manner in which the Church communicates is so very important in this and the coming age. It is embarrassingly clumsy to assume that by speaking down to younger people we are relating to them on their level. Better Mozart, Purcell, or William Byrd than a poor, stale attempt to be a contemporary musician. Any parent can tell you that fashions are exactly that; they are out of date faster than you can say, "But I only bought you that CD a month ago." Yet it has been repeatedly shown that reverence, tradition, and the unchanging worship of the Church is supremely attractive to young people. The future Church in worship must be the eternal Church in worship.

Peter Murphy, executive director of the Secretariat of Evangelization and Catechesis of the U.S. Conference of Catholic Bishops, believes that there are seven essentials to what is known as the new evangelization.

"It's not new in content, but new in energy and approach. The New Evangelization re-proposes the faith to a world longing for answers to life's most profound questions. It's a call to share Christ and bring the Gospel, with renewed energy and through

ever-changing methods, to new and different audiences. *It begins with personal conversion.* The New Evangelization begins internally and spreads outward. We are called to deepen our own faith in order to better share it with others. Then-Cardinal Joseph Ratzinger described this in the Jubilee Year 2000 as daring to have faith with the humility of the mustard seed that leaves up to God how and when the tree will grow. Conversion to Christ is the first step. *It's for believers and non-believers alike.* Philadelphia Archbishop Charles Chaput, OFM Cap., recently observed that the most difficult people to evangelize are the ones who think they've already been converted. So whether it's someone at Mass every Sunday, an inactive Catholic or someone for whom religion is not part of life, the New Evangelization invites all people to discover faith anew. *It's about a personal encounter with Jesus Christ.* Before a person can share Christ with others, they must first experience Christ in their own life. The New Evangelization is about promoting a personal encounter with Christ for all people, wherever they are in their lives. Whether that means finding faith for the first time or spreading the Good News, the most authentic and effective efforts are the ones closest to Christ. *It's not an isolated moment, but an ongoing practice.* Personal conversion and the encounter with Christ is an ongoing experience that lasts a lifetime. Catholics are blessed to encounter their Lord and Savior, Jesus Christ in the Sacraments. Catholics are called to live in a way that reflects the love of Christ. God's love is shared with our neighbors through caring for the poor and welcoming those who feel distant from God. *It's meant to counter secular culture.* G.K. Chesterton wrote that 'each generation is converted by the saint who contradicts it most.' The New Evangelization responds to Western society's ongoing move away from religion by urging Catholics to enthusiastically share Christ in word and through the credible witness of their lives. This is why Pope Benedict encourages Catholics to study the lives of the saints during the Year of Faith and learn from their example. *It's a priority for the Church.* Blessed Pope John Paul II made it a major priority of his 26-year pontificate. Continuing this, Pope Benedict launched the Pontifical Council for Promoting New Evangelization in 2010 and made it the theme of the 2012 Synod of Bishops."[13]

Not a bad manifesto for the future Church to nail to the doors of the church of secularism or watered-down Catholicism. As to how Catholics themselves will worship in the future Church, this is more significant than it might seem. In early 2013, a group of bishops from the Italian region of Tavoliere met with Pope Francis. Such meetings are held only every five years and are an opportunity for local episcopal leaders to explain to the Holy Father the most pressing and challenging concerns that they have. The great dilemma for these men, it seemed, was not the state's increasingly aggressive war against the Church, not the slaughter of myriad unborn babies, not the loss of countless souls through militant secularism disguised as Catholic education, not same-sex marriage ravaging western Europe and North America, but the fact that many sincere, devout Catholics in their area were increasingly attracted to the traditional Mass – the Mass, of course, that was heard by the great martyrs and doctors of the Church throughout history.

The meeting was reported on by the Italian centre-right newspaper *Il Foglio* – The Sheet – under the headline "The old mass is not to be touched, the Jesuit Pope wrong-foots everyone." The newspaper reported, "Then it was the turn of the bishop of Conversano and Monopoli, Domenico Padovano, who recounted to the clergy of his diocese how the priority of the bishops of the region of Tavoliere had been that of explaining to the Pope that the mass in the old rite was creating great divisions within the Church. The underlying message: Summorum Pontificum should be cancelled, or at least strongly limited. But Francis said no. Mgr Padovano explained that Francis replied to them saying that they should be vigilant over the extremism of certain traditionalist groups but also suggesting that they should treasure tradition and create the necessary conditions so that tradition might be able to live alongside innovation."

The incident says a great deal about Pope Francis and also about the bishops in question, who are not of course unique in this regard within the modern Church. They tried to exploit a new Papacy and were under the absurd impression that because the Holy Father wants to reach out to the poor and marginalized and is not himself a particular devotee of traditional liturgy, he is somehow liberal and modernist. Not at all. He's Catholic! But it reveals some of the divisions that will likely develop still further within the future Church. The middle point, and the likely resolution that will develop, will be an attachment to reverence rather than Latin. The Mass is about the body and blood of Christ, and since the 1960s there has been a disturbing degree of badly written and delivered evangelical singing, and of priests confusing flippancy with relevance. There is far worse of course: clown masses, so-called inclusive masses, liturgical dancing. These are not about Jesus and Catholicism at all, and little more than opportunities for the self-obsessed to parade themselves in front of an altar that is designed exclusively for the Son of God.

One of the triumphs of Latin is that it prevents such perversion and heresy, and guarantees pristine orthodoxy. But we have moved on, and as splendid and even desirable as is the old Mass, it is simply not going to become the norm. But we must make sure that any Catholic who wants it must have it made available to them. Remember, Vatican II merely said that where there was sufficient demand, the Mass should be provided in the vernacular. Within a year it was almost impossible to hear it in Latin, not because congregations demanded it but because a generation of liberal clergy in their love of democracy and equality told those in the pews what to do and how they should behave.

Bishop Dominique Rey summarized the essence of the New Evangelization in its liturgical context clearly and cleverly in his opening address to the Sacra Liturgia Conference in Rome in June 2013 when he explained that the New Evangelization is not so much an idea or a program but a demand that we all know Christ on a more personal level. He stressed that the only way to fulfil this relationship – and this is essential Catholicism – is through the Sacred Liturgy. If that liturgy is not correct, he continued, the relationship will suffer as a consequence. "That is why our celebration of the liturgy is so important. We must maximize, not limit, the action of Christ in the liturgy. If I change or re-create the Church's liturgy according to my own wishes or a subjective ideology, how can I be sure that what I am doing is truly His work? Whereas, if I faithfully celebrate that which the Church has given to us – and celebrate it as beautifully as possible – I am assured that I am a servant of Christ's action, a minister of His sacred mysteries, not an obstacle in his path. Each of us, ordained ministers, religious and lay men and women, are called to this fidelity and respect for Christ, for His Church and for her liturgical rites. And that is why liturgical formation is crucial. I must obtain 'from within' as it were, the conviction that Christ is indeed at work in the Church's sacred rites. I must immerse myself in this privileged dynamic and discover its ways. This will bring me to the person of Jesus Christ again and again. And this will enable me to bring Christ to others."

There we have it. The future Church is likely to generally have the balance about right. Interest in the Latin Mass is growing and its fiercest enemies tend to be older bishops who are gradually giving way to better, more understanding, more Catholic men. Outright persecution of the old Mass still exists but has declined enormously, and general respect and awe for the Eucharist is increasing exponentially, miraculously. This is the splendid, majestic, and seamless garment extending from the time of Christ – His body and blood – to the present, to the future Church. It's the all, the everything, and evangelization, ecumenism, and all that are related are mere ripples to this rock of salvation thrown into the waters of human existence. This, then, is the essence of the future Church, and as long as Catholics hold to it there will be no defeats that last longer than passing moments.

VIII

POPE FRANCIS

THE PHRASE "We are expecting great things" has varying definitions according to who says it and who hears it. That the secular and non-Catholic world expected great things from Pope Francis means something rather different from the Catholic world expecting the same. Part of this is what we should describe as the law of diminishing Papal nastiness. Pope John Paul II was roundly condemned by the mainstream media when he was alive, but once he was dead and succeeded by Pope Benedict XVI, these same journalists recalled and sighed alas for the time of a gentler, kinder Pope. Then Pope Francis was chosen, and for the briefest of honeymoons he was thought to be a reforming Jesuit who would, the media seemed to imply in their speculative fantasies, transform the Church into an especially lenient and liberal kindergarten. Then he spoke of sin quite a lot, then emphasized that life began at conception and that euthanasia was unacceptable, then refused to affirm same-sex marriage, and as quickly as the love festival started it abruptly stopped. He was, ran the first attack, a collaborator with the authoritarian juntas of 1980s Argentina. When this nonsense evaporated, they opted for the alternative plan of indifference. Oh dear. What a disappointment the Holy Father was to them.

Actually, he has pointed the way to what the future Church will be like in all sorts of ways and pursued a *via media*, a middle road, that has not always pleased left and right wings of the Church, but delighted the massive middle. In June 2013, he made it abundantly clear that the present and future Church was not a cafeteria where we chose what we wanted and rejected what didn't appeal. The food came as one, unified, holistic meal. "This is salvation: to live in the consolation of the Holy Spirit, not the consolation of the spirit of this world. No, that is not salvation, that is sin. Salvation is moving forward and opening our hearts so they can receive the Holy Spirit's consolation, which is salvation. This is non-negotiable. You can't take a bit from here and a bit from there? We cannot pick and mix, no? A bit of the Holy Spirit, a bit of the spirit of this world... No! It's one thing or the other."

Referring to the Gospel of Matthew and the Beatitudes, he said: "They are the new commandments. But if we do not have a heart open to the Holy Spirit, they will seem silly. 'Just look, being poor, being meek, being merciful will hardly lead us to success.' If we do not have an open heart and if we have not experienced the consolation of the Holy Spirit, which is salvation, we cannot understand this. This is the law for those who have been saved and have opened their hearts to salvation. This is the law of the free, with the freedom of the Holy Spirit. Today we can now ask the Lord for the grace to follow Him, but with this freedom. Because if we want to follow him with our human freedom alone, in the end we become hypocrites like the Pharisees and Sadducees, those who quarreled with him. This is hypocrisy: not allowing the Spirit to change our hearts with His salvation."

There was a forlorn hope from the left of the Church that a Jesuit and a non-European would make it easier for dissenters to do exactly what they like best, but they had misjudged the man and misunderstood his Church. This came into sharp focus the following month, June, when Pope Francis entertained a group of priests and nuns from his native Latin America.

Although what was said was not officially recorded – and the people present at the meeting later tried to distance themselves from having revealed what was discussed – it became obvious that here was the Pope speaking from his heart, off the cuff, and without the filter of officialdom. "In the Curia there are holy people, truly, there are holy people. But there's also a current of corruption – there's that, too, it's true. . . . The 'gay lobby' is spoken of, and it's true, that's there . . . we need to see what we can do. The reform of the Roman Curia is something that almost all the cardinals sought in the congregations before the Conclave. I sought it myself. [But] I can't do the reform myself, these matters of management. . . . I'm very disorganized, I've never been good in this. But the cardinals of the commission are going to carry it forward."[1]

He continued: "I'll share two worries of mine. One is a pelagian current that's in the church at this time. There are certain restorationist groups. I know them as I took to receiving them in Buenos Aires. And you feel like you've gone back 60 years! Before the Council . . . you feel like it's 1940 again. . . . One anecdote, only to illustrate this – not to make you laugh – I took it with respect, but it bothered me; when they [the cardinals] elected me, I received a letter from one of these groups, and they told me: 'Holiness, we offer you this spiritual treasure: 3,525 rosaries.' Why they didn't say 'we're praying for you,' let's wonder . . . but this [thing] of taking account [of prayers] . . . and these groups return to practices and disciplines I lived – not you, none of you are old – to things that were lived in that moment, but not now, they aren't today. The second [worry] is over a gnostic current. These pantheisms . . . they're both currents of elites, but this one is of a more formed elite. I knew of one superior general who encouraged the sisters of her congregation to not pray in the morning, but to give themselves a spiritual bath in the cosmos, such things. . . . These bother me because they lack the Incarnation! And the Son of God who became our flesh, the Word made flesh, and in Latin America we have this flesh being shot from the rooftops! What happens to the poor, in their sorrows, that is our flesh. The Gospel is not the *ancien regime*, nor is it this pantheism. If you look to the outskirts – the indigent . . . the drug addicts! The trade [trafficking] of persons . . . That's the Gospel. The poor are the Gospel. . . . There's something else that bothers me, but I don't know how to read it. There are religious congregations, very, very small groups, a few people, [who tend to be] very old. . . . They don't have vocations, that I know, [whether] the Holy Spirit doesn't want them to continue, maybe they've finished their mission in the church, I don't know. . . . But there they are, clinging to their buildings, clinging to money. . . . I don't know why this happens, I don't know how to read it. But I ask you to be worried about these groups . . . The handling of money . . . is something that needs to be reflected on."[2]

There is a lot here to unpack, and some of it may be open to question, but it's vital for any understanding of Pope Francis and of the future Church, because here is a man speaking as he feels. While various officials fluffed and fussed about all this, there were no concrete denials, and only a cloud of unknowing that floated around it all. In other words, what was claimed to have been said almost certainly was said.

First, a gay lobby in the Vatican. No serious person with any interest in or knowledge of the Church and of Rome has ever doubted the existence of an influential collective of priests and bureaucrats in the Vatican who have allowed their homosexuality to become the prime factor in their spirit and psyche. The specifics here are important. We all know priests who have same-sex attractions, but whose celibacy, spirituality, faithfulness, and Catholicism dominate their character and oblige all other personal aspects to become largely irrelevant. What the Church proclaims, however, is that we are all so much more than our mere sexuality, and one of the tragedies of modernity is that it is reductive, minimizing the grandeur of humanity to the small and the relatively petty. In other words, while sex is profoundly important as part of God's loving plan for His creatures and their continued existence, and while sin is sin, there are many forms of brokenness. So we shouldn't assume that "gay lobby" refers to hard-working, sacrificing, devout clergy who struggle successfully and valiantly against sexual temptation.

What Pope Francis surely meant here are people who act out their perversions, use the Church as a cover for their weakness, and allow their sexuality to influence their convictions and theology, and then apply those beliefs to greater Church governance. This is immoral and damaging on a whole variety of levels, and it is vital that these men are removed from positions of influence as soon as possible, particularly if they operate as a collective and directly try to influence the Church. Most Catholics have known priests whose awareness of their homosexual desires and absolute resistance to acting on them has made them stronger in their faith, but there are also men who never intended a life of celibacy or gave up the struggle with hardly any resistance at all. Remember, the vast majority of the abuse cases that have caused the Church, and the victims, so much pain were of a homosexual nature, with more than 80 per cent of those abused being not children but post-pubescent teenaged boys. Many of the abusers were also involved in adult homosexual relationships.

The future Church must not, cannot, indulge in a witch hunt, but in an informed, sensible, and compassionate cleansing of Rome, the curia, and the inner sanctum of the Church of those who are not living as proper Catholics and proper clergy. It's long overdue, and what surprised so many commentators was how little outrage, even of the artificial kind, resulted from the Pope's comments, and how few screams of "homophobia!" Perhaps when the self-evident is so pronounced, denial seems pointless. As discussed in the chapter on same-sex marriage, the coming years will bring the Church into direct conflict with the state over same-sex marriage, as nation after nation adopts the policy. Marriage is a Sacrament, sexual union has a specific purpose, and the Church can no more affirm homosexual behaviour than it can abandon Jesus Christ. So we have two immutable assumptions and cultures on a direct collision course. It's why we have to be able to speak and act with a clear conscience and with one voice. No hypocrisy, no sabotage, no fifth column. The Pope's comment alone will have sent shock waves through parts of the Church, in Rome as well as internationally, and that will have done some good. Now let's watch as the new generation of well-formed, orthodox young men take their places in the clergy, new bishops take charge of dioceses, and the future Church takes shape.

But there was much more than this in what Pope Francis said. Corruption in the curia. Once again, this has long been assumed but seldom discussed in any detail. The word *curia* really means court and derives from the royal courts of Europe. The Roman Curia in the Vatican is where the various office and departments of state are located, and they are known as "dicastaries." That the Curia demands reform is not a new concept, and as far back as the eleventh century, Pope Gregory VII undertook fundamental changes, followed in the sixteenth century by the reforming work of the Council of Trent, and more recently after Vatican II in the 1960s, which was supposed to have opened some windows – too often, however, this allowed the undesirable to enter and the precious to be pushed out. Briefly, reform has not worked up to now, but it looks likely that with the public statements from the Pope that the Curia has to change, and with the semi-private admissions that corruption is within the Curia culture, this is the start of a new curia for a future Church.[3]

There are four main areas where change is essential: financial, sexual, personal, and ethical; these areas of change can themselves be divided into two other subsections: systemic and fundamental reform, and a change in the way the existing structures are managed. Money is a problem and its abuse a temptation in every walk of life, and the Church is, sadly, no different. While it's a myth, an anti-Catholic fantasy, to believe that the clergy are wealthy and that bishops enjoy lavish lifestyles, the Vatican and its civil service do have to deal with large amounts of money, investments, and all that this entails and implies. Pope John Paul brought Cardinal Edmund Szoka into the Vatican to transform its archaic accounting system, and Pope Benedict in 2011 set the scene for the future Church when he commanded that the Vatican accept the financial standards of Moneyval, the Committee of Experts on the Evaluation of Anti-Money Laundering Measures and the Financing of Terrorism, under the auspices of the Council of Europe. This was a quite revolutionary step, in that it allowed an outside, secular agency to watch over Rome's finances, just as that agency did any other nation-state.

There seems to be relatively little financial corruption within the Curia, but there is certainly financial incompetence and still too little transparency. It is not enough for the future

Church to be financially clean, even pristine, but also it must be seen as such. What Popes John Paul and Benedict initiated and Pope Francis has continued is certain to be made complete in the coming years.

The sexual abuse scandal and its consequences are dealt with elsewhere in greater depth.

Within the Curia, however, there are genuine problems that are difficult to expose and thus deal with because they involve not only harassment but the added complication in an overwhelmingly male environment of these harassment problems being related to homosexuality. The gay lobby mentioned earlier is a reality, as are gay men in the clergy and the lay Curia. Any form of sexual advance, blackmail, pressure, or intimidation must be dealt with immediately and relentlessly and cannot be hidden from public scrutiny. The Church has learned from bitter experience that attempts to hide internal difficulties often cause more harm than the difficulties themselves.

The Curia is composed of fallible people, with ambitions, resentments, and anxieties. Pope Francis has spoken of the destructive nature of careerism, and most Catholics have encountered a priest or two who is clearly eager for high office and who often find it, too. There is nothing more enervating to a member of the Church than to see an obviously ambitious priest climbing higher and higher, while his humbler and better brothers are denied promotion. They might not want it, of course, but nevertheless it is unfair. It breeds resentment, and it encourages infighting. Differences of opinions and even theology are inevitable in the Curia, but a greater sense of fraternity and solidarity has to be fostered and encouraged.

There has to be a better system of efficiency and the guarantee of ethical standards. In recent years, we have seen a culture of leaking documents and revealing secrets and classified information to the press, sometimes for mere personal gain or as a price paid to satisfy a blackmailer, and sometimes – more often the case – so as to try to influence a particular decision or embarrass a Cardinal or even a Pope of whom a Curia official disapproves. This has to be prevented. The Italian media is notorious for its willingness to print and broadcast gossip and scandal, the Italian public renowned for its love of conspiracy theories and revelations, particularly when they concern the Vatican and the Papacy. The leaks must be sealed, and anybody who breaks the oaths of his position must be dismissed.

In general terms, the Curia has to be dragged several hundred years into the modern and future age. Just a few years ago, the Vatican seemed to have discovered new media, around a decade after the rest of the world had found it. Catholic bloggers had transformed Catholic media, and some of the most popular – who are invariably orthodox or conservative – in particular had attracted hundreds of thousands of followers each, millions as a group. There are hundreds of them, driving the Church conversation and having made themselves essential reading to anyone who wants to know what is going on within the Church. The Vatican decided to bring Catholic bloggers together but, instead of inviting the best and brightest, and most popular, opted for a dull grouping of safe, bland types who had never offended anyone and were embarrassingly irrelevant. The real thing, the prestigious Catholic bloggers, were forced to assemble an alternative conference. It's a typical example of a civil service and court rooted in a past age, and Pope Francis seems to be the man to begin if not complete the change that has to take place.[4]

He also spoke of the need to reach out to the poor, and he stresses this point time and time again. Catholicism is the Church of the poor, the poor are the Gospel, poverty must be challenged, it is a sin to ignore the hungry and the needy, and so on. There is nothing new in this, and the Church has long been the friend, often the only friend, of the poor. But Pope Francis is making this relationship, this spiritual marriage, a key motif of his pontificate and of the future Church.

Shortly after becoming Pope, he told the Church: "Poverty in the world is a scandal. In a world where there is so much wealth, so many resources to feed everyone, it is unfathomable that there are so many hungry children, that there are so many children without an education, so many poor persons. Poverty today is a cry. We all have to think if we can become a little poorer, all of us have to do this. How can I become a little poorer in order to be more like Jesus, who was the poor Teacher? First of all I want to tell you something, tell all you young persons: don't let yourselves be robbed of hope. Please, don't let it be stolen from you. The worldly spirit, wealth, the spirit of vanity, arrogance, and pride . . . all these things steal hope. Where do I find hope? In the poor Jesus, Jesus who made himself poor for us. And you spoke of poverty. Poverty calls us to sow hope. This seems a bit difficult to understand. . . . Look, you can't speak of poverty without having experience with the poor. You can't speak of poverty in the abstract: that doesn't exist. Poverty is the flesh of the poor Jesus, in that child who is hungry, in the one who is sick, in those unjust social structures. Go forward; look there upon the flesh of Jesus. But don't let well-being rob you of hope, that spirit of well-being that, in the end, leads you to becoming a nothing in life. Young persons should bet on their high ideals, that's my advice. But where do I find hope? In the flesh of Jesus who suffers and in true poverty. There is a connection between the two."[5]

It couldn't be much clearer than this. The natural constituency for the future Church is the poor. Obviously when Scripture speaks of poverty, it also means those who are poor in spirit, who are spiritually empty, but we assume these will always be people to whom the Church has to reach. But the literally poor are something different. It is simply untrue to believe that the Church has never been in the business of aiding and feeding the hungry and powerless, and beyond the famous saints and renowned pioneers, there are legions of clergy, monks, nuns, and laypeople who have devoted all or part of their lives to such work. When the monasteries were destroyed in England in the sixteenth century, contrary to what was once believed, the latest historical research shows just how much the monks did for the poor and homeless in Tudor society, and how neglected and rejected these people were after their sanctuaries of food and succor were obliterated.[6] Through the succeeding centuries, the Catholic Church was often the only place for the poor to turn, and on a systemic level it was often and sometimes exclusively the Church that established hospitals, schools, and kitchens. In other words, do not believe the anti-Catholic propaganda that dominates the narrative.

In the second half of the twentieth century, however, and especially after the 1960s, liberation theology came into being and swamped the discourse regarding the Church and the poor. This was disastrous, because in typical Marxian manner it is assumed that the only way for a Catholic to truly stand with the poor was through revolution and class struggle, sometimes of a violent kind, and so alienated millions of Catholics and their non-Catholic supporters who wanted to help the poor individually and work toward structural change, but did not see this as being achieved through radical socialism, and quite rightly saw

Marxism as secular, flawed, and failed, and ultimately God-hating and anti-Church. Pope Francis's Jesuit order was particularly culpable in this, and he was obliged to work out his own deeply Catholic yet non-socialist response to poverty. This is what we see now in his homilies and letters, as he hammers away at the Church, and the future Church, being the parent, the brother, the sister of the poor the world over. Socialism has failed the poor, and governments of various stripes have not managed to address the deeper problems of poverty. The future Church will evangelize to the poor, transform their lives economically, and save their lives spiritually.[7]

Some of his ideas can sound quite radical, but then the Church is not focused on complacency. He has spoken of a "tyranny" where people are judged by their ability to consume, argued that money should be made to "serve" people, not to "rule" them, and called for limits to financial speculation: "While the income of a minority is increasing exponentially, that of the majority is crumbling" and "The worship of the golden calf of old has found a new and heartless image in the cult of money and the dictatorship of an economy which is faceless and lacking any truly human goal." He pulled no punches when he told the world, "The Pope loves everyone, rich and poor alike, but the Pope has the duty, in Christ's name, to remind the rich to help the poor, to respect them, to promote them." So it's a future Church not always seeing eye to eye, or trading dollar to dollar, with the world's wealthy and powerful.

The Pope also spoke in the private meeting of some religious orders having more money than vocations, and this is painfully clear. It's hard to know how self-analytical he was being, because the Society of Jesus, the Jesuits, the order that produced Pope Francis himself, is a prime example of a Catholic institution that was once vibrant and prolific, and now cannot even hope to replace its numbers. The same is true of several other older orders of priests, but the situation is quite startling when it comes to nuns. The new orders such as Sisters of Life and Sisters of Charity are attracting young women in large numbers, and their defining characteristic is orthodoxy and a strong sense of traditional Catholicism. They live, however, in makeshift and often inadequate houses, while the older and moribund orders operate what have become virtual old people's homes in grand settings, and then sell off the property when there is simply nobody left. It is terribly sad to see these once grand and visible collections of nuns consisting of seventy-year-old women caring for eighty-year-old women and then disappearing completely. For some of these orders, it is simply time to go. This, surely, is what Pope Francis meant when he spoke of his concerns and worries. The future Church will see continued growth in new orders and new movements, and also the birth – inevitably – of groups we have yet to see. Right now, there is enormous strength in Sant'Egidio, the Neocatechumenate, Focolare, Communion and Liberation, Opus Dei, Schönstatt, Regnum Christi, and others, all immensely successful in a variety of areas and charisms. This seems to be a springtime for such movements, and judging by the enthusiasm of young Catholics in universities in particular, we can only imagine what is to come.

Lastly, he gave examples of what in secular terms we would call the hard right and hard left of the Church, and implied that Catholicism, the future Church, was a grand, great essence, a quintessence in fact, of Christ and His Church – nothing more, nothing less. Mere Catholicism. This is less a political than a theological division, and the sides are hardly equal. While the vast majority of Catholics lead their religious lives without giving too much concern to issues beyond the general, there are those who are convinced that the Church has lost its way or has to find a new direction. In defence of more orthodox or conservative Catholics, they look to valid tradition and genuine Catholicity, and they have been marginalized and even persecuted for the best part of half a century. They have watched as Catholic education has been emasculated and secularized, and liberal careerists have reached positions of enormous influence, and even stood by in horror as repeated attempts have been made to destroy the meaning of the Mass. They have struggled for sincerity, fought for faithfulness. Those on the left, on the other hand, have usually tried to reshape the Church in their own image, invariably one of materialistic and misunderstood social justice, and an expunging of the spiritual, timeless, grace-filled, and – in the best sense – religious from the Catholic world.

When it comes to more conservative Catholics, the Pope was speaking here, it seems, less of the mass of faithful Catholics who pray for a restoration of genuine Catholicism than of those who place form above content, and those who perhaps allow pedantry to take the place of a relationship with Christ. By orthodox Catholicism, the faith of the future Church, we don't mean silly affectation and self-conscious traditionalism. Good Lord, there are some believers who seem more Miss Havergal than dynamic Catholic, some churches where the miasma of languour and lace is positively choking. This is not the Pope Francis approach, and wasn't the John Paul II spirit, nor the Pope Benedict impetus. At the centre of the new Church is reverence, a reverence once disregarded and misplaced in the ridiculous race to be "relevant." We are in the world but not of the world, we use the new media but do not allow it to seduce us, we embrace the best of modernity but are aware of its threat, we look for dignified and precise English rather than an archaic language that excludes, we change the present rather than live in the past. An image that comes to mind is of the post-Reformation Church in the six-teenth century. There were some Catholics who looked to the restoration of medievalism, something that could never occur. Then there were the younger, reformed, and educated Catholics who worked for an intensely faithful but refreshed Catholicism. We know many of them now as saints, but they were the new orthodox of their time. We are not made for the bunker or the ghetto, but for the shining light on the hill. Pope Francis leads the Church at arguably one of the most important and exciting stages of Catholic history, and the Church of the future will look back to the first decades of the twenty-first century as a time of immense change and a new dawn. As such, it can be frightening and challenging to older and older-thinking conservatives as well as liberals seeking change for its own sake. One of the ironies here is that laypeople, often championed by critics of Church authority, are some of the leading figures in this return to ortho-doxy and truth. But this has always to be undertaken and under-stood as an extension, a reflection, of God and Christ, not of individuals and their personal comforts.

In a far more public display, and in a surprising first decree of a liturgical nature of his pontificate, only a few months after he became Holy Father, Pope Francis decided that the name of St. Joseph should be added to the Eucharistic Prayers ii, iii, and iv, as they appear in the third typical edition of the Roman Missal, after the name of the Blessed Virgin Mary. Vatican radio reported: "Exercising his paternal care over Jesus, Saint Joseph of Nazareth, set over the Lord's family, marvelously fulfilled the office he received by grace. Adhering firmly to the mystery of God's design of salvation in its very beginnings, he stands as an exemplary model of the kindness and humility that the Christian faith raises to a great destiny, and demonstrates the ordinary and simple virtues necessary for men to be good and genuine followers of Christ. Through these virtues, this Just man, caring most lovingly for the Mother of God and happily dedicating himself to the upbringing of Jesus Christ, was placed as guardian over God the Father's most precious treasures. Therefore he has been the subject of assiduous devotion on the part of the People of God throughout the centuries, as the support of that mystical body, which is the Church."

The thrust of this is twofold. First, while the importance of the clergy cannot be overstated, and the future Church has to stress the essential nature of the Sacrament of holy orders, the place of Catholic laymen will become central to the vitality of the Church in years to come. Organizations such as Opus Dei realized this long ago, with relatively few priests within the group but so many men as fathers and centres of families. In other words, the other kind of fathers. Second, it confirms the future Church as the defender of family and of parents – in this case, fathers in particular – as being crucial to the health and well-being of a civilized and balanced society. Fathers have been under attack and the subject of waves of mockery for decades in Western media and culture, and Pope Francis's liturgical statement drew a line in the sand, or more accurately built a wall in the desert of anti-family hysteria.

During the G8 meetings in London in 2013, British prime minister David Cameron, temporary president of the G8, wrote to Pope Francis, explaining the economic policies of the world's economic powers, and outlining how the G8 wants "fairer taxes, freer trade and greater transparency." The Pope replied, and much of what he said could form a manifesto for the future

Church's approach to world economics and international politics: "If this topic is to attain its broadest and deepest resonance, it is necessary to ensure that all political and economic activity, whether national or international, makes reference to man. Indeed, such activity must, on the one hand, enable the maximum expression of freedom and creativity, both individual and collective, while on the other hand it must promote and guarantee their responsible exercise in solidarity, with particular attention to the poorest. . . . Yet the fundamental reference to man is by no means lacking, specifically in the proposal for concerted action by the Group to eliminate definitively the scourge of hunger and to ensure food security. Similarly, a further sign of attention to the human person is the inclusion as one of the central themes on the agenda of the protection of women and children from sexual violence in conflict situations, even though it must be remembered that the indispensable context for the development of all the afore-mentioned political actions is that of international peace."[8]

He then spoke specifically about war in the Middle East and how peace is an essential prerequisite for the protection of women, children, and other innocent victims, and to begin the war against hunger and poverty. He continued: "Therefore concern for the fundamental material and spiritual welfare of every human person is the starting-point for every political and economic solution and the ultimate measure of its effectiveness and its ethical validity. Moreover, the goal of economics and politics is to serve humanity, beginning with the poorest and most vulnerable wherever they may be, even in their mothers' wombs. Every economic and political theory or action must set about providing each inhabitant of the planet with the minimum wherewithal to live in dignity and freedom, with the possibility of supporting a family, educating children, praising God and developing one's own human potential. This is the main thing; in the absence of such a vision, all economic activity is meaningless.

"In this sense, the various grave economic and political challenges facing today's world require a courageous change of attitude that will restore to the end (the human person) and to the means (economics and politics) their proper place. Money and other political and economic means must serve, not rule, bearing in mind that, in a seemingly paradoxical way, free and disinterested solidarity is the key to the smooth functioning of the global economy. I wished to share these thoughts with you, Prime Minister, with a view to highlighting what is implicit in all political choices, but can sometimes be forgotten: the primary importance of putting humanity, every single man and woman, at the centre of all political and economic activity, both nationally and internationally, because man is the truest and deepest resource for politics and economics, as well as their ultimate end."

If we read such a letter from a secular political leader, where we would we place that statesman politically and economically? The question is worth asking, because what tends to stagnate political and economic change is the placing of labels, often fruitlessly and pointlessly, on positions and policies. If they are perceived as being right wing, the left is obliged to oppose them. If they are considered left wing, the right has to oppose them. The unique position of the Pope, of the Church, of the future Church, is that for good or bad it cannot be seriously labelled in such a way, and so its statements carry a moral weight almost impossible to equal in a purely political context. There are no accidents in conclave decisions, and Pope Francis is here at such a time to start a new era in the Church's influence on the world. He is challenging even to many Catholics and would perhaps be the first to admit, to boast, that he is not here for our comfort.

Father Christopher Jamison, director of the National Office for Vocation in Britain, put it thus: "As Pope Francis said in his address to the press: 'Christ remains the centre, not the Successor of Peter. . . . Without him, Peter and the Church would not exist or have reason to exist.' So how will Christ be at the centre for Pope Francis? The classic theological description of Christ is Prophet, Priest and King. While all these three aspects of Christ's life will be present in a papacy, one usually emerges as dominant. In Blessed John Paul II's ministry, the prophetic element was to the fore. The Christ whom he preached literally made nations tremble and empires crumble. Similarly, in his final illness he offered us Christ crucified as a prophetic challenge and as an affirmation of the culture of life. Turning to Pope Benedict, we see a papacy characterized strongly by Christ the High Priest. In his emphasis on greater dignity in the liturgy, combined with his outstanding sermons and speeches on a wide variety of themes, Pope Benedict presented in his ministry Christ as priest and, derived from that, Christ as teacher city."[9]

The right man at the right time? The future Church will answer that question.

CONCLUSION

IN JANUARY 2013, Father C.J. McCloskey, a priest of the prelature of Opus Dei, wrote that the United States was no longer a Christian country. Whether we liked it or not, he said, the country had some of the most liberal abortion laws in the world, the morning-after pill was available at the local pharmacy, and girls were being exposed to such things at progressively younger ages. "Pornography is the most profitable and watched form of 'entertainment.' Marriage is being redefined not as a covenant between man and wife, with one of its purposes being the procreation of children, but as more or less whatever one wants it to be: men contracted to men, women to women, and maybe bestiality down the road. I shudder to think of where it may all end, especially when our collapsing population is already at the lowest rate in American history. And who can disingenuously doubt that universal euthanasia for the incurable will become common with the help of our new 'health' plan? But wait – is there hope? Yes, even though God only promised a rose garden to Adam and Eve (and they blew it, as we well know, seeing that we still suffer the consequences). However, we have the promise that someday, after the final judgment, we will inhabit a new heaven and a new earth with the company of the Holy Trinity, Our Lady, and all the saints. I look forward to it, but in the meantime we have work to do. The future is always bright for faithful Catholics, and it is an honor and a privilege to be foot soldiers in the Battle for Life in this country. All is not lost for us and our country, since HE is on our side. Blessed Pope John

Paul the Great (who we may piously hope may be proclaimed a saint before the year is out!) has told us what to do. The question to ask ourselves is: Are we doing what he told us – with faith, hope, and charity, and without faltering?"[1]

Therein lies the dilemma for the future Church, not just in the United States but throughout the Western world. These are, I suppose, what are mockingly termed "first world problems," but it's much more difficult to respond to poverty, war, and injustice if the centre of the Church in North America and Europe is so mired in difficulties. And the particular difficulty that has to be dealt with by the future Church is the abuse crisis, otherwise whatever the Church says and does is open to criticism by its opponents. Thing is, to a very large extent the abuse crisis already has been dealt with. When we discuss the horrific episode, it is extraordinarily difficult to sound fair and sympathetic. Because if we are the former, we seem to lack in the latter; if the latter, we often neglect the former. To describe what happened is sometimes assumed to be a defence or even some sort of vile justification. There are still some cases coming to light, but even when the grime has finally been left behind, there will still be people who wish to beat the Church with the stick of sexual abuse.

So we have to be bold, and hope that stating truth will offend only those who have no sense of balance when it comes to Catholicism. Denial is immoral, obfuscation as bad. Perhaps as much as 2 per cent of clergy were directly or indirectly involved, the typical victim was a teenage boy, and for the most part the reaction of bishops and bureaucracy was to order the abuser to change parish, seek counselling, and never repeat the crime.[2]

Today we cringe when we hear of such a pathetic response. But this was standard secular, psychiatric advice at the time, and that given to school boards, sports organizations, and other religious bodies. We now know better, but it's significant that while those other groups are not taken to task for not doing enough, the Church is attacked for its callousness. Good Lord, the double standard and the tendentious history are almost overwhelming!

Of course there were men in authority who chose to do nothing out of their own sexual brokenness, but they were a tiny number. It was panic rather than perversion that characterized the worst of the response, and that is something for which we should all be deeply ashamed. But there is surely no other group of men and women on earth that have done so much since all of this to put matters right, to show contrition, and to make the Church arguably the safest place for a young person to be.

Tragically, this is not the case for all institutions. In the United States in particular, the influence of teachers' unions has meant that in public education some abusers have not been dismissed and are still teaching. Abuse is a reflection of the broken status of the human person. We are fallen, damaged, in need of repair. It says nothing about the Roman Catholic Church, other than this is why we need the Church, to guide us back to the ways of God, Christ, and holiness. If it were a result of celibacy, there would be no abuse in non-Catholic churches or hockey teams; if it were due to an all-male clergy, there would be no abuse in families – where, obscenely, it is actually at its highest.

These are just excuses used by unscrupulous critics with an agenda to attack Catholicism. They often seem more concerned with using the abuse issue to attack the Church than with caring for the victims of the actual abuse. I remember meeting a man in his late twenties who had been sexually molested by a priest. The priest later took his own life. I expected to meet an angry, Catholic-hating person, but instead had the privilege of spending time with a devout, peaceful Roman Catholic.

"I was abused by a man, not by the Church. He used the Church to further his lust, and I see the Catholic Church as being as much a victim in all this as I am," he said, making me feel extremely inadequate. "Yes, I was in despair at first, and yes, I refused to go to Mass. Then I returned, because what I found there was not some cruel abuser, but the saviour who had been abused, tortured, killed for me and for all of us. He knew me, wept for me, made me feel that I wasn't alone. If I let that awful, abusive man take me away from the Church I've let him win again and again. He's not going to do that."

As well as sinners among us, there are saints. So, so many saints.

In fact, the Pope had written a long letter to the Irish Church as early as March 2010. This came after prolonged reform of the church in Ireland, prosecution of criminals, removal of priests, and the introduction of practices intended to prevent further abuse. To some critics of Catholicism the letter may as well never have existed as it simply didn't fit in with their caricature of an indifferent Papacy unconcerned with the suffering of the vulnerable. Actually it said, among other things:

"Dear Brothers and Sisters of the Church in Ireland, it is with great concern that I write to you as Pastor of the universal Church. Like yourselves, I have been deeply disturbed by the information which has come to light regarding the abuse of children and vulnerable young people by members of the Church in Ireland, particularly by priests and religious. I can only share in the dismay and the sense of betrayal that so many of you have experienced on learning of these sinful and criminal acts and the way Church authorities in Ireland dealt with them.

"No one imagines that this painful situation will be resolved swiftly. Real progress has been made, yet much more remains to be done. Perseverance and prayer are needed, with great trust in the healing power of God's grace. . . . At the same time, I must also express my conviction that, in order to recover from this grievous wound, the Church in Ireland must first acknowledge before the Lord and before others the serious sins committed against defenceless children. Such an acknowledgement, accompanied by sincere sorrow for the damage caused to these victims and their families, must lead to a concerted effort to ensure the protection of children from similar crimes in the future.

"As you take up the challenges of this hour, I ask you to remember 'the rock from which you were hewn.' (Is 51:1) Reflect upon the generous, often heroic, contributions made by past generations of Irish men and women to the Church and to humanity as a whole, and let this provide the impetus for honest self-examination and a committed programme of ecclesial and individual renewal. It is my prayer that, assisted by the intercession of her many saints and purified through penance, the Church in Ireland will overcome the present crisis and become once more a convincing witness to the truth and the goodness of Almighty God, made manifest in his Son Jesus Christ."[3]

It's difficult to know how much more powerful and absolute the Pope could have been. Writing in the New York Times, John Allen, the doyen of Vatican correspondents, who is respected by critics as well as supporters of the Church due to his balanced and layered reporting, stated that Pope Benedict was "a major chapter in the solution." He continued, "After being elected Pope, Benedict made the abuse cases a priority. One of his first acts was to discipline two high-profile clerics against whom sex abuse allegations had been hanging around for decades, but had previously been protected at the highest levels. He is also the first pope ever to meet with victims of abuse, which he did in the United States and Australia in 2008. He spoke openly about the crisis some five times during his 2008 visit to the United States. And he became the first pope to devote an entire document to the sex abuse crisis, his pastoral letter to Ireland."

In Britain in 2010, the then newly appointed Archbishop of Westminster, Vincent Nichols, argued that Pope Benedict was "the one above all else in Rome that has tackled this thing head on." In the *Times* of London he said, "When he was in charge of the Congregation for the Doctrine of the Faith he had important changes made in Church law: the inclusion in canon law of internet offences against children, the extension of child abuse offences to include the sexual abuse of all under 18, the case by case waiving of the statute of limitation and the establishment of a fast-track dismissal from the clerical state for offenders. He is not an idle observer. His actions speak as well as his words." Yet none of this stopped people such as the late Christopher Hitchens from writing in *Slate* that the Pope was "obstructing justice on a global scale." Benedict's whole career, he said, "has the stench of evil – a clinging and systematic evil that is beyond the power of exorcism to dispel." This from someone regarded by his atheist and Catholic-basher friends as an original and profound thinker. It is entirely possible to be critical of Pope Benedict but no serious person who has read his books and speeches and studied his views and actions on delicate themes such as anti-Semitism, the Third World, poverty, war, or globalization could regard Hitchens's views on the Pope as anything other than cruel, flippant, or dumb. Yet he was given full pages in reputable newspapers and magazines to give us ever-more repetitive versions of his propaganda.

The latest reports and figures only go to proving what informed commentators already assumed or knew to be the case. In the most recent annual audit of abuse in the Catholic Church, documented in the *Report on the Implementation of the Charter for the Protection of Children and Young People,* from the Secretariat of Child and Youth Protection, under the auspices of the National Review Board of the United States Conference of Catholic Bishops, only six credible cases of abuse allegations by priests were reported for the year 2012 in the entire United States. To put this in context, there are more than 40,000 Catholic priests in the country. This represents the lowest number of cases since 2004, when the audit was instituted. It is, by the way, independently and scrupulously checked, and open to outside and public scrutiny. The 2012 report was audited by the private company StoneBridge Business Partners. There is no reason at all to believe that these figures would be dissimilar to those in any other country.[4]

One would have thought that after so much media attention given to the abuse crisis, ostensibly because so many journalists were deeply concerned at the fate of young people and wanted the situation to be repaired and rectified, there would be widespread reporting of the good news and the successful work of the Catholic Church. What a surprise, then, when we heard hardly anything about this report and its findings! Only three newspapers that were not part of the Catholic media covered the report, and they were all small and with a limited circulation. The *Press-Register* in Alabama, the *Rapid City Journal* in South Dakota, and the *Georgia Bulletin.* When we consider how much ink, how many pages, how many columns and editorials were devoted to the abuse issue, and how many reporters and columnists spent hours covering it, it is breathtaking that this vital part of the story was never reported. The *New York Times* and *Boston Globe* in particular, so eager to report actual and doubtful priestly crimes or indiscretions, suddenly became so quiet and reserved. It's all too easy, and often so commonplace as to be irritating, to complain that the Church is not treated fairly in and by media, but in this case the lack of mention of what was, in effect, the conclusion, the finale, the denouement, of the abuse crisis was utterly shameful.

The story goes further. Almost half of all of the priests who were named – some remained anonymous and unidentified – in 2012 had been dead for some time, most of those accused in 2012 were dead, missing, or had already been laicized or punished in some other form, and three-quarters of the abuse charges in 2012 date from before 1985. This is a record that shows quite clearly that the Church has dealt with the issue, that the issue is more historical than current, and that the future Church is likely to have a minor challenge on its hands, and one nowhere near as difficult and numerous as, for example, public education or organized sport. Part of the problem that the future Church will face is that any explanation of the abuse crisis is seen as obfuscation, any reasonable analysis dismissed as a justification. It's entirely understandable that journalists would be sensitive to the claims of victims, but not every alleged victim is to be believed, and many have been exposed recently as people who are emotionally needy or financially unscrupulous. It puts the Church and its defenders in an extremely difficult position, and it's made worse by lawyers who are determined to exploit the situation, and activists with an agenda.

SNAP, the Survivors Network of Those Abused by Priests, once did fine and vital work. That is no longer the case. Lutheran minister Russell E. Saltzman has written, "I no longer believe the Survivors Network of Those Abused by Priests (SNAP) is in any way *primarily* an advocacy organization for sexual abuse victims. Instead, I think it is more a noisy little group that hates the Roman Catholic Church and has discovered a way of making a living off the victimization others have suffered." It's a point made by others, both inside and outside of the Church, but SNAP is still regarded as the arbiter of the situation by perhaps the majority of mainstream journalists. Media Report is an information and reporting source that deals extensively with accusations of abuse and had years of exposing the guilty and also defending the innocent. "In truth, when it comes to protecting one's own image rather than children, SNAP itself has been shown to do this very same thing. The group's National Director David Clohessy refused to call the police back in the early 1990s when he fully knew that his priest brother Kevin was sexually abusing innocent boys, an action by Clohessy which possibly jeopardized the safety of countless children. And just a couple years ago, SNAP founder Barbara Blaine actually wrote a passionate letter on behalf of a SNAP psychiatrist arrested with over 100 images of kiddie porn on his computer. So much for protecting kids. Indeed, it would appear that children are much safer in the arms of the Catholic Church than under the supervision of the leaders at SNAP." Yet it is guaranteed that whenever questioned are asked about the future Church, one of the first will be along the lines of how will it deal with the abuse crisis. No need, it had and it did.[5]

A more authentic challenge is declining numbers in attendance in churches in the West. There are numerous reasons for this, but one is the decline in the Catholicity of ostensibly Catholic education. Very few people who have gone through even more than a decade of Catholic education go on to lead their lives as practising Catholics. Even accepting the understandable percentage of those who simply reject what they have been taught, and the pressures they face once they leave a Catholic environment, the numbers just don't add up. In other words, they are not actually being educated and formed as Catholics in the first place. As we discussed earlier, this necessitates a fundamental reform if not scrapping of Catholic education as we know it, at the high school and university level. But beyond that is the inability to reach out to people in an age of myriad temptations and distractions. One example the future Church should look at is the archdiocese of Vancouver, in British Columbia. This is a large, vibrant, and cosmopolitan city of more than 600,000 people, with many growing suburbs on its edges, and a generally liberal culture. For some years now at the political level, the province has had liberal and social democratic governments. Yet between 2007 and 2012, the archdiocese has added 37,000 new members, and the trend is even more encouraging.

According to Archbishop J. Michael Miller, immigration from Catholic countries such as the Philippines accounts for some of the increase, but far from all. "Our largest numbers of those who were not baptized as children, but who were received into the church as adults, comes largely from the Korean and Chinese and East Asian communities in rather significant numbers. That spurs on the growth. . . . We have parishes in the archdiocese, where on an average Sunday it has 5,000 people. At Easter, it has more than 7,000 on the day." As for Pope Francis and the growth of the future Church, the Archbishop believes that "his example will spur us to make sure that if it slipped away from our consciousness, that it should move back into a central place. In the building we're in now, upstairs at night there's 104 men sleeping. It's the largest men's shelter in British

Columbia. We feed hundreds of people down on the Lower East Side. We have a large outreach in prison ministries. The big questions for the church are homelessness, addiction, marginalization, attentiveness to the incarcerated, and the need for a broader understanding of restorative justice."

He is also a highly orthodox and faithful man and has influenced his priests and the culture of the archdiocese accordingly. "I don't think it's the church's role to adapt to modern society. It is true that the decline in practice has taken place. In the West, statistics can verify that. The decline is certainly something to be paid attention to. And B.C. is one of the areas where there is the largest percentage of the population that reports either agnostic or atheistic beliefs. We believe that the fundamental message is entrusted or given to us. It's not something we're free to change or adapt because we like or don't like it. If we believe it comes from a revelation, our duty is to proclaim that, to do it as attractively as possible . . . but not at any cost."

As for the issues of abortion and the Church's opposition to same-sex marriage, the latter particularly difficult for younger Catholic to defend and accept, "they are slightly different issues. It's really hard to find a real practising Catholic who thinks abortion is okay, someone who goes to church every week. On the question of gay marriage, there's probably not the same unanimity, although I've never . . . heard any Catholic . . . suggest that they would see it [gay marriage] as really marriage, as a sacramental marriage, which is marriage for Catholics. The biggest challenge is always the fundamental one that the church is always facing: How do you talk about God, in a world which seems in some ways, particularly in the West, to be uninterested in that question. It's not that it [society] has articulated objections, it's just indifferent. The superficiality of modern life – that is the biggest enemy."[6]

Archbishop Miller makes the point that others have stressed, that tampering with belief and diluting practice is no long-term answer at all, and possibly even positively dangerous. While there is a great deal written about evangelizing those who have left Catholicism and the Church for a secular life, the future Church needs to deal with the phenomenon of Catholics not abandoning Christ but changing their form of Christianity. There are Catholics who find the teachings of the Church too rigid and embrace any number of liberal Protestant denominations, but these churches have little long-term future and attract Catholics often for less than deeply theological reasons: people want to divorce and remarry, they want to use contraceptives, they are gay or their children are gay. More of a problem are those evangelical churches, and in particular Pentecostal or charismatic churches, that offer warmth, certainty, emotional highs, networks of support, and a conservatism that some Catholic parishes have rejected. Remember, people who leave the Catholic Church for other forms of Christianity rather than secularism or for theological rather than personal, pragmatic reasons generally want more and not less orthodoxy.

So quite clearly facile attempts to be "relevant" or "fashionable" are not really the solution, and there is perhaps too much said and written about what is known as the new evangelization. Many if not most things with the word *new* in them are an admission that the person making the statement isn't quite clear what to do. While the future Church has to master blogs, social media, the Internet, and the latest in communication technology, it is still what is written on these vehicles of conversation rather than the vehicles themselves that matter most. Pride in having set up a Catholic blog is laughable; there are countless blogs out there, and to stand out and make any sort of difference or impression, the writers and the writing have to reach out, connect, attract. If we look at the numbers, the hits, the blogs and sites that do the best – constantly and consistently – are those that offer orthodox and traditional Catholicism, at their best with a twist of humour, and even a flavour of the sardonic and satirical. "Oh Lord, isn't it great that the Bishop has a blog" is almost certainly not what we want to hear and is simply not enough.

The future Church must explain why it thinks what it thinks. The Sacraments and the Church's teaching are spiritually clear, intellectually compelling, theologically crisp. Yet this is seldom transmitted from the pulpit, and one of the absolutes of the future Church is the teaching of better preaching in the seminaries. It is not easy for a priest with all of his other work and commitment to write and deliver a good sermon, but then not everybody is called to be a priest. It's not about politics, it's not about feel-good anecdotes, and it's certainly not about personal opinions. It's about clear, insightful, understandable, even amusing explanations of why the Church is the Church and why it holds to what it believes to be true. Feelings are not enough in all this, because feelings by their nature are transitory and will change. If I have had a particularly good sleep, an especially good cup of coffee, I may feel extremely good about my faith and my religion; if I have argued with my wife, had a bad time at work, I may feel like giving the whole thing up. Feelings are not the answer. And this leads to some of the challenges of Charismatic Catholicism, which certainly has its place in the future Church but must not be allowed to dominate worship and liturgy. The Church is international, and not a Catholic version of American evangelicalism.[7]

But there is also another dynamic to this. As much as the numbers in the West can be increased, the future Church will not be centred in its historical heartland. Author and journalist John

Allen has written, "In 1900, there were 459 million Catholics in the world, 392 million of whom lived in Europe and North America. Christianity 100 years ago remained an overwhelmingly white, first world phenomenon. By 2000, there were 1.1 billion Catholics, with just 380 million in Europe and North America, and the rest, 720 million, in the global South. Africa alone went from 1.9 million Catholics in 1900 to 130 million in 2000, a growth rate of almost 7,000 percent. This is the most rapid and sweeping demographic transformation of Catholicism in its 2,000 year history. Sao Paolo, Jakarta and Nairobi will become what Leuvein, Milan and Paris were in the Counter Reformation period, meaning major centers of pastoral and intellectual energy. Different experiences and priorities will set the Catholic agenda as leaders from Africa, Asia and Latin America rise through the system, reshaping the texture of church life."

This is inevitable. When the Catholic author and journalist Hilaire Belloc wrote his *Europe and the Faith* in 1920, he could write quite accurately that the history of the continent was largely a Catholic history, and that one could not understand Europe without understanding Catholicism, and vice versa. He also implied that this would always be the case, and that Europe was a Christian entity and the heartland of Catholicism. Not so. The history of the Church shows us that while North Africa may have once been the homeland of the faith, it was conquered by Islam and is hardly Christian at all any longer. Constantinople once contained the greatest Church in the world and was the centre of eastern Christianity. It is now the largest city in Muslim Turkey, and that church was turned into a mosque, then a museum, and now may well become a mosque once again. It will certainly never be a church. Europe today is under threat from secularism, relativism, liberalism, indifference, and Islam. There is no indication that any of this will change radically in the days of the future Church. The Muslim diaspora in Europe, and in particular in heavily Catholic countries such as France, Belgium, even parts of Germany, Italy, and Spain, the cult of materialism, and its little sister atheism emerging in formerly Catholic nations such as Ireland, Croatia, and Poland, and state power and control of freedom of speech throughout western Europe all join to put enormous pressure on the Church. The positive aspect of this is that those who remain Catholic tend to become solidly and enthusiastically Catholic, but it also means that the lukewarm will become cold, and that evangelism will become difficult, even at times impossible in the traditional sense. Traditional but not historical, in that there have been times in Catholic history when it has also been effectively impossible.[8]

But measured by numbers and influence, the future Church will often be a different colour, from a different culture, speaking a different language. That is worrying to the nostalgic, but not at all to the genuinely Catholic. It's not confined to Catholicism, of course, and Anglicanism, for example, has its future in Africa and Asia, where it is strongest and also most conservative. So a future Church that may look a little different but will in every important respect be the Church of the past. The truths may be told in a different form, may be expressed in a new format, and even communicated in a way that some of us will find novel and challenging, but they will be the same truths. For ever and ever. Amen.

NOTES

INTRODUCTION

1. www.catholicanswers.com
2. George Weigel, *Evangelical Catholicism* (Basic Books, 2013).

CHAPTER ONE
MARRIAGE

1. Manya A. Brachear. *Chicago Tribune*, May 26, 2011.
2. Sally Thompson. *Christian Science Monitor*, August 27, 2010.
3. Kevin J. Vanhoozer, *Dictionary for Theological Interpretation of the Bible* (Baker Book House, 2005).
4. *New International Version Bible*, Paul's Letter to the Romans, 1, 18–32.
5. *New International Version Bible*.
6. Romano Penna. *L'Osservatore Romano*, April 2, 2009.
7. Robert Gagnon, *The Bible and Homosexual Practice: Texts and Hermeneutics*, Abingdon, 2002.
8. Ibid.
9. Ian Ker, *John Henry Newman: A Biography* (Oxford, 2009).
10. Mike Aquilina, The Fathers of the Church, Our Sunday Visitor, 2006.
11. Ibid.

CHAPTER TWO
ABORTION AND BIRTH CONTROL

1. Dr. Brian Clowes, *The Facts of Life* (HLI, 1997).
2. Robert P. George and Christopher Tollefsen, *Embryo: A Defence of Human Life* (Doubleday, 2008).

3. "New Feminism: Angela Elizabeth Lanfranchi, M.D.,"
   http://www.newfeminism.co/author/angela-lanfranchi/.

4. Scott Klusendorf, *The Case for Life* (Crossway, 2009).

5. U.N. Population Database, 2008.

6. Mary Eberstadt. *First Things*, August/September 2008.

7. John Paul II, *The Theology of the Body* (Pauline, 1997).

8. Dr. Chris Kahlenborn, *Breast Cancer* (OMS, 2000).

CHAPTER THREE
EUTHANASIA

1. Dr. Brian Clowes, *The Facts of Life* (HLI, 1997).

2. John Carey, *The Intellectuals and the Masses* (London, 1992).

3. Jack Kevorkian, *Prescription Medicide* (Prometheus Books, 1991).

4. Dyingwithdignity.ca

5. Frank Pavone, *Ending Abortion* (Catholic Books, 2006).

6. Pope John Paul II, Crossing the Threshold of Hope (Random House, 1995).

7. Wesley J. Smith, *Forced Exit: Euthanasia, Assisted Suicide and the New Duty to Die* (Encounter Books, 1997).

CHAPTER FOUR
CHURCH AND STATE

1. Archdiocese of Boston, press release, May 10, 2013.

2. Jorge Mario Bergoglio and Abraham Skorka, *On Heaven and Earth: Pope Francis on Faith, Family, and the Church in the Twenty-First Century* (Random House, 2013).

3. NBCnews.com, January 31, 2012.

4. Robert Royal. *The Catholic Thing*, August 30, 2009.
   www.catholicthing.org.

6. *Catholic Insight*, February 2006.

7. *Priests for Life*, June 18, 2013.

8. *Lifesite News*, November 22, 2010.

9. Peter Ackroyd, *The Life of Thomas More* (Anchor, 1999).

CHAPTER FIVE
FEMALE ORDINATION AND MARRIED PRIESTS

1. *Catholic Herald*, March 27, 2013.

2. Jorge Mario Bergoglio, *On Heaven and Earth: Pope Francis on Faith, Family, and the Church in the Twenty-First Century* (Random House, 2010).

3. John R. Willis, *The Teachings of the Church Fathers* (Ignatius Press, 2002).

4. Carl J. Sommer, *We Look for a Kingdom* (Ignatius Press, 2007).

5. *Catholic World Report*, 2005.

6. *Daily Telegraph*, August 11, 2010.

7. *Huffington Post*, July 19, 2013.

8. John R. Willis, *The Teachings of the Church Fathers* (Ignatius Press, 2002).

9. *National Catholic Reporter*, August 9, 2008.

CHAPTER SIX
PAPACY

1. Stephen K. Ray, *Upon This Rock* (Ignatius, 1999).

2. Ibid.

3. John R. Willis, *The Teachings of the Church Fathers* (Ignatius Press, 2002).

4. Ibid.

5. Austin Flannery, *Vatican Council II: The Conciliar and Postconciliar Documents* (Costello Publishing, 1975).

6. Charles A. Coulombie, *A History of the Popes* (MJF Books, 2003).

7. Willis, *The Teachings of the Church Fathers*.

8. Ibid.

9. Cristina L.H. Traina, "Blackmail or Corruption? Catholics Respond to the Vatican's 'Gay Lobby.'" *Aljazeera* magazine, February 13, 2013.

CHAPTER SEVEN
ECUMENISM AND NEW EVANGELIZATION

1. The Regensburg lecture, September 12, 2006.
2. Author interview, January 2010.
3. *Jerusalem Post*, May 6, 2013.
4. Giorgio Paolucci and Camille Eid, *111 Questions on Islam: Samir Khalil Samir, S.J. on Islam and the West* Ignatius, 2008.
5. Rabbi David G. Dalin, *The Myth of Hitler's Pope* (Regnery, 2005).
6. Ibid.
7. *Huffington Post*, July 11, 2013.
8. Author's visit to Germany, 2010.
9. *First Things*, May 1994.
10. Joint International Commission for Theological Dialogue Between the Catholic Church and the Orthodox Church, October 2007.
11. *Il Messaggero*, June 2013.
12. *Catholic Insight*, January 2012.
13. Peter Murphy, www.usccb.org.

CHAPTER EIGHT
POPE FRANCIS

1. Rorate Caeli, blog entry, June 11, 2013. http://rorate-caeli.blogspot.com/search?updated-max=2013-06-18T00:00:00Z2.
2. Ibid.
3. John Allen Jr., *All the Pope's Men: The Inside Story of How the Vatican Really Thinks* (Doubleday, 2003).
4. Ibid.
5. *National Catholic Reporter*, June 7, 2013.

6. Eamon Duffy, *The Stripping of the Altars: Traditional Religion in England, 1400–1580* (Yale, 1992).

7. Christopher Rowland, *Cambridge Companion to Liberation Theology* (Cambridge University Press, 2007).

8. www.zenit.org, June 17, 2013.

9. *Catholic Herald*, March 29, 2013.

CONCLUSION

1. Fr. C. John McCloskey III, "Post Christian America," *The Catholic Thing*, August 19, 2012.

2. Catholic League, May 10, 2013.

3. Vatican papal letter, March 19, 2010.

5. www.themediareport.com, May 15, 2013.

6. Ibid.

7. *BC Catholic*, November 5, 2012.

8. John Allen Jr., *The Future Church: How Ten Trends are Revolutionizing the Catholic Church* (Doubleday, 2009).

9. Catholic News Service, April 10, 2013.

BIBLIOGRAPHY

WHAT FOLLOWS IS A LIST of published and readily available works I consulted for this book, but it is by no means definitive. The bibliographies from each book themselves should and can be used for further reading in any specific area.

Allen, John L. Jr. *Opus Dei* (Doubleday, 2005).

Armstrong, Regis. *Writings for a Gospel Life* (St. Paul's, 1994).

Bergoglio, Jorge Mario, and Abraham Skorka. *On Heaven and Earth: Pope Francis on Faith, Family, and the Church in the Twenty-First Century* (Random House, 2013).

Blankenhorn, David. *The Future of Marriage* (Encounter Books, 2007).

Bunson, Matthew. *Pope Francis* (Our Sunday Visitor, 2013).

Burleigh, Michael. *Earthly Powers* (HarperCollins, 2005).

Burleigh, Michael. *Sacred Causes* (HarperCollins, 2007).

Carroll, Warren. *A History of Christendom*, 5 vols. (Christendom Press, 1987—2010).

Cathechism of the Catholic Church (Chapman, 1994).

Chaput, Charles J. *Render Unto Caesar* (Doubleday, 2008).

Chesterton, G.K. *Heretics* (1905, London).

Chesterton, G.K. *The Everlasting Man* (Ignatius, 1993).

Clowes, Brian. *The Facts of Life* (HLI, 1997).

Coffin, Patrick. *Sex Au Naturel* (Emmaus Road, 2010).

Collins, Roger. *Keepers of the Keys of Heaven* (Basic, 2009).

Craughwell, Thomas J. *Pope Francis: The Pope From the End of the Earth* (St. Benedict Press, 2013).

Crean, Thomas. *A Catholic Replies to Professor Dawkins* (Family Publications, 2007).

D'Souza, Dinesh. *What's So Great About Christianity* (Regnery, 2007).

Dalin, David G. *The Myth of Hitler's Pope* (Regnery, 2005).

Daniel-Rops, H. *The Church in an age Age of Revolution* (Dent, 1965).

Duffy, Eamon. *The Stripping of the Altars* (Yale, 2005).

Erlandson, Gregory, and Matthew Bunson. *Pope Benedict XVI and the Sexual Abuse Crisis* (Our Sunday Visitor, 2010).

George, Robert P., and Christopher Tollefsen. *Embryo: A Defence of Human Life* (Doubleday, 2008).

Gilbey, A.N. *We Believe* (The Saint Austin Press, 2003).

Guarducci, Margherita. *The Primacy of the Church of Rome* (Ignatius, 2003).

Hogge, Alice. *God's Agents* (2006, Harper).

Jenkins, Philip. *Pedophiles and Priests* (Oxford, 2001).

John Paul II. *The Theology of the Body* (Pauline, 1997).

Jones, E. Michael. *Degenerate Moderns* (Ignatius, 1993).

Kahlenborn, Chris. *Breast Cancer* (OMS, 2000).

Keating, Karl. *Catholicism and Fundamentalism* (Ignatius, 1988).

Ker, Ian. *Mere Catholicism* (Emmaus Road, 2006).

Klusendorf, Scott. *The Case for Life* (Crossway, 2009).

Knox, Ronald. *The Belief of Catholics* (London, 1927).

Kreeft, Peter. *The Snakebite Letters* (Ignatius, 1991).

Kurzman, Dan. *A Special Mission* (Da Capo, 2007).

Longenecker, Dwight. *More Christianity* (Our Sunday Visitor, 2002).

Madrid, Patrick. *Pope Fiction* (Basilica, 2005).

Madrid, Patrick. *Why Is That in Tradition* (Our Sunday Visitor, 2002).

Muggeridge, Anne Roche. *The Desolate City* (McClelland & Stewart, 1986).

Nathanson, Bernard N. *Abortion Papers: Inside the Abortion Mentality* (Frederick Fell, 1983).

Nathanson, Bernard N. *The Hand of God: A Journey from Death to Life by the Abortion Doctor Who Changed His Mind* (Regnery, 2001).

Nichols, Aidan. *Christendom Awake* (Eerdmans, 1999).

Pham, John-Peter. *Heirs of the Fisherman* (Oxford, 2004).

Reisman, Judith A. *Kinsey: Crimes and Consequences* (The Institute for Media Education, 2000).

Ripley, Francis. *This Is the Faith* (TAN, 2002).

Rumble, Fr., and Fr. Carty. *Radio Replies,* 3 vols. (TAN, 1979).

Sheed, Frank. *Theology and Sanity* (Ignatius, 1978).

Sommer, Carl J. *We Look for a Kingdom* (Ignatius 2007).

Tornielli, Andrea. *Francis: Pope of a New World* (Ignatius, 2013).

Urs von Balthasar, Hans. *Dare We Hope That All Men Be Saved?* (Ignatius, 1988).

von Kempis, Stefan, and Philip F. Lawler. *A Call to Serve: Pope Francis and the Catholic Future* (SPCK Publishing, 2013).

Waugh, Evelyn. *Edmund Campion* (Ignatius, 2005).

Weigel, George. *Letters to a Young Catholic* (2006, Gracewing).

Weigel, George. *The Courage to Be Catholic* (Basic, 2002).

Weigel, George. *Witness to Hope* (Collins, 1999).

Willis, John R. *The Teachings of the Church* (Ignatius, 2002).

Woods, Thomas E. *How the Catholic Church Built Western Civilization* (Regnery, 2005).

Zolli, Eugenio. *Before the Dawn* (Sheed & Ward, 1954).

ACKNOWLEDGEMENTS

THERE ARE MANY PEOPLE whom I should thank for encouraging me to write this book, especially so soon after my previous two volumes in a similar vein – *Why Catholics Are Right*, and *Heresy: Ten Lies They Spread About Christianity*. First is my editor and publisher, Doug Pepper, who while not a Catholic has encouraged me in so many ways and made this book, and the previous two, possible. Thanks must also go to everybody at Random House. Many friends, both within and a long way outside of the Church, have been supportive in ways they perhaps don't even imagine. Special thanks to Canada's Cardinal Collins, Father Tim Finegan, Father Philip Cleevely, Walter Hooper, Raymond Arroyo, Chris Corkery, Jim O'Leary, David Beresford, John Hayes MP, Francis Wheen, Paul Godman, Father Ian Ker, Peter Stockland, Stephen Hayhurst, and most of all to my wife, Bernadette. To the people whose names I have forgotten, fear not because you might be better off in years to come not having been mentioned in a book discussing the future of Catholicism; easier to deny any links that way!